The third book in the Master Comprehension series builds on the skills introduced in previous books and adds an additional skill: recognizing details. Master Comprehension helps children enjoy learning through entertaining and informative puzzles, articles, poems and other activities about dinosaurs and other high-interest topics. The 5 skills covered in this book are listed on the next page in the Glossary.

Table of Contents

Glossary

Comprehension. Understanding what is read.

Following Directions. Doing what the directions say to do.

Inference. Using logic to figure out what is unspoken but evident.

Main Idea. Finding the most important points.

Recognizing Details. Being able to pick out and remember the who, what, when, where, why and how of what is read.

Name: _____

Main Idea: A Lizard-like Dinosaur

Millions of years ago, many kinds of dinosaurs roamed the earth. The name of one kind of dinosaur was Iguanodon. (Here is how to say it: Ee-gwan-eh-don.) The Iguanodon looked like a giant lizard. It had tough skin. The Iguanodon's skin must have felt like leather! Iguanodons ate plants.

Directions: Answer these questions about Iguanodons.

1. The main idea is:

    The Iguanodon's skin was like leather.

    The Iguanodon was a plant-eating dinosaur with tough skin.

2. What kind of food did Iguanodons eat?

_____

_____

3. What animal living today did the Iguanodon look like?

_____

_____

_____

Sizes Of Dinosaurs

There were many sizes of dinosaurs. Some were as small as dogs Others were huge! The huge dinosaurs weighed 100,000 pounds. Some dinosaurs ate meat – including other dinosaurs. Some dinosaurs, like the Iguanodon, ate only plants. Meat-eating dinosaurs had sharp teeth. Plant-eating dinosaurs had flat teeth. If you had lived long ago, would you have gotten close enough to look at their teeth?

Directions: Answer these questions about dinosaurs.

1. What size were the small dinosaurs?

_____

_____

2. How much did the big dinosaurs weigh?

_____

_____

3. Name 2 things the different kinds of dinosaurs ate.

1) _____   2) _____

4. What kind of teeth did meat-eating dinosaurs have?

_____

_____

5. What kind of teeth did plant-eating dinosaurs have?

_____

_____

Name: _____

Making Inferences: Dining Dinosaurs

Brontosaurus dinosaurs lived in the swamps. Swamps are water areas where many plants grow. Here are the names of the other kinds of dinosaurs that lived in the swamps. The way to say their names is shown inside the ( ). Diplodocus (dip-low-dock-us), Brachiosaurus (Bracky-o-saur-us) and Cetiosaurus (Set-e-o-saur-us). These dinosaurs had small heads and small brains. They weighed 20 tons or more. They grew to be 60 feet long! These animals did not need to have sharp teeth.

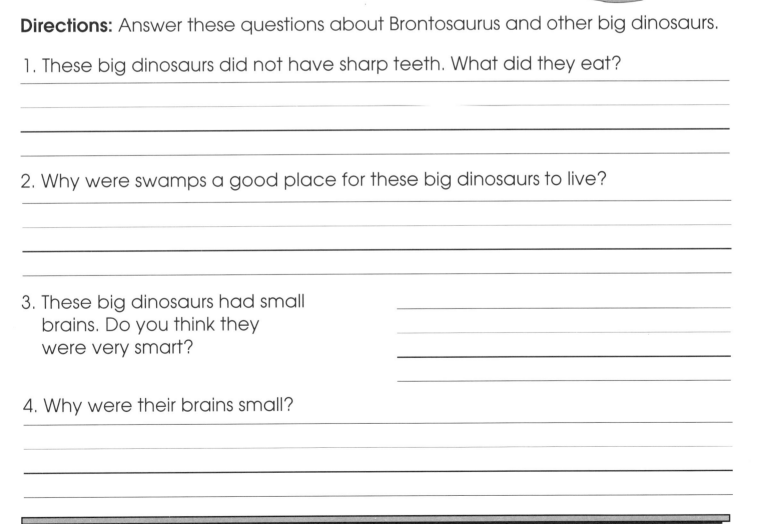

Directions: Answer these questions about Brontosaurus and other big dinosaurs.

1. These big dinosaurs did not have sharp teeth. What did they eat?

_____

_____

2. Why were swamps a good place for these big dinosaurs to live?

_____

_____

3. These big dinosaurs had small brains. Do you think they were very smart?

_____

_____

4. Why were their brains small?

_____

_____

Name: _____

Dinosaurs Were Cold-Blooded

Like snakes, dinosaurs were cold-blooded. Cold-blooded animals cannot keep themselves warm. Because of this, dinosaurs were not very active when it was cold. In the early morning they did not move much. When the sun grew warm, the dinosaurs became active. When the sun went down in the evening, they slowed down again for the night. The sun warmed the dinosaurs and gave them the energy they needed to move about.

Directions: Answer these questions about dinosaurs.

1. Why were dinosaurs inactive when it was cold?

_____

_____

2. What times of day were the dinosaurs active?

_____

_____

3. What times of day were the dinosaurs not active?

_____

_____

4. Why did dinosaurs need the sun?

_____

_____

_____

Name: _____

Tyrannosaurus Rex

One of the biggest dinosaurs was Tyrannosaurus Rex. (Here is how to say his name: Ty-ran-oh-saur-us Recks.) The dinosaur walked on its two big back legs. It had two small, short front legs. From the top of his head to the tip of his tail, Tyrannosaurus measured 50 feet long. His head was 4 feet long! Are you taller than this dinosaur's head? Tyrannosaurus was a meat-eater. He had many small sharp teeth. His favorite meal was a smaller dinosaur that had a bill like a duck. This smaller dinosaur lived near water.

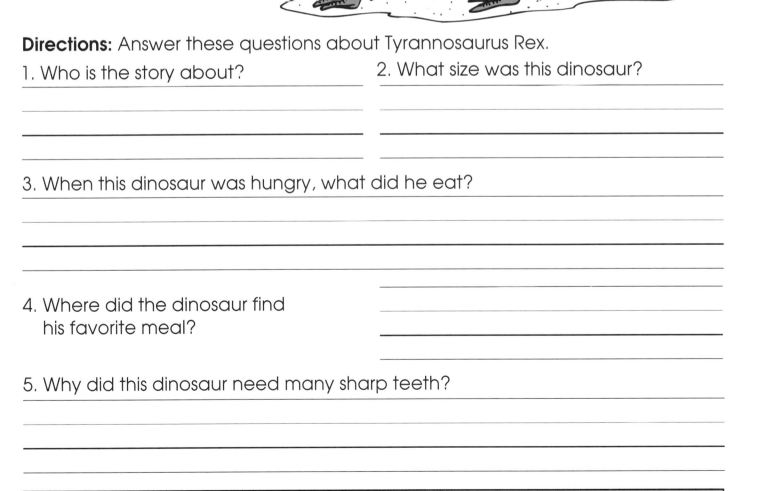

Directions: Answer these questions about Tyrannosaurus Rex.

1. Who is the story about?

_____

_____

_____

2. What size was this dinosaur?

_____

_____

3. When this dinosaur was hungry, what did he eat?

_____

_____

_____

4. Where did the dinosaur find his favorite meal?

_____

_____

5. Why did this dinosaur need many sharp teeth?

_____

_____

_____

Name: _____

When Dinosaurs Roamed

Dinosaurs roamed the earth for 125 million years. Can you imagine that much time? About 40 years ago, some people found fossils of dinosaur tracks in Connecticut. Fossils are rocks that hold the hardened bones, eggs and footprints of animals that lived long ago. The fossil tracks showed that many dinosaurs walked together in herds. The fossils showed more than 2,000 dinosaur tracks!

Directions: Answer these questions about fossils.

1. What did the people find in the fossils?

2. In what state were the fossils found?

3. How many tracks were in the fossils?

4. What did the tracks show?

5. How long did dinosaurs roam the earth?

Name: _____

Main Idea: Dinosaur Models

Some people can build models of dinosaurs. The models are fakes, of course. But they are life-size and they look real! The people who build them must know the dinosaur inside and out. First they build a skeleton. Then they cover it with fake "skin." Then they paint it. Some models have motors in them. The motors can make the dinosaur's head or tail move. Have you ever seen a life-size model of a dinosaur?

Directions: Answer these questions about dinosaur models.

1. The main idea is:

Some models of dinosaurs have motors in them.

Some people can build life-size models of dinosaurs that look real.

2. What do the motors in model dinosaurs do?

_____

_____

_____

3. What is the first step in making a model dinosaur?

_____

_____

_____

4. Why do the dinosaur models look real?

_____

_____

_____

Name: _____

Review

There are no dinosaurs alive today. They became extinct millions of years ago. This was before people lived on earth. (Say the word this way: ex-tinkt.) When animals are extinct, they are gone forever. No one knows exactly why dinosaurs became extinct. Some scientists say that a disease may have killed them all. Other scientists say a huge hot rock called a comet hit the earth. The comet caused a big fire. The fire killed the dinosaurs' food. Still other scientists believe that the earth grew very cold. The dinosaurs died because they could not keep warm. Many scientists have ideas, but no one can know for sure just what happened.

Directions: Answer these questions about dinosaurs becoming extinct.

1. Why is it not possible to know what caused all the dinosaurs to die?

_____

_____

_____

2. The main idea is:

    The dinosaurs died when a comet hit the earth and caused a big fire.

    There are many ideas about what killed the dinosaurs, but no one knows for sure.

3. What does extinct mean?

_____

_____

_____

4. Who are the people with the ideas   _____
   about what happened to dinosaurs?   _____

                                          _____

Name: _____

Athletes' Nicknames

Directions: Read about nicknames. Then work the puzzle.

Do you have a nickname? Nicknames are the silly names people call each other. Sometimes nicknames are mean. Usually nicknames are nice. Most people do not mind if their friends make up a nice nickname for them. Many athletes have nicknames. Have you heard of a football player named "Refrigerator" Perry? He is very big! How about a basketball player named "Magic" Johnson? Can you guess why he got that nickname?

Across

2. "Refrigerator" is very _____ .
4. The silly names that people call each other.
5. "Magic" Johnson is a basketball _____ .

Down

1. Johnson's nickname.
3. "Refrigerator's" last name.

Name: _____

Kareem Abdul-Jabbar

Have you heard of a basketball star named Kareem Abdul-Jabbar? When he was born, Kareem's name was Lew Alcindor. He was named after his father. When he was in college, Kareem changed his religion from Christian to Muslim. That is when he took the Muslim name of Kareem Abdul-Jabbar.

Directions: Answer these questions about Kareem Abdul-Jabbar.

1. What was Kareem Abdul-Jabbar's name when he was born?

_____

_____

2. Who was Kareem named after?

_____

_____

3. When did Kareem become a Muslim?

_____

_____

4. When did he change his name to Kareem Abdul-Jabbar?

_____

_____

Name: _____

More About Kareem Abdul-Jabbar

Kareem Abdul-Jabbar grew up to be more than 7 feet tall! Kareem's father and mother were both very tall. When he was 9 years old, Kareem was already 5 feet 4 inches tall. Kareem was raised in New York City. He went to Power Memorial High School and played basketball on that team. He went to college at UCLA. He played basketball in college, too. At UCLA, Kareem's team lost only 2 games in 3 years! After college, Kareem made his living playing basketball.

Directions: Answer these questions about Kareem Abdul Jabbar.

1. Who is the story about?
_____

_____

2. What is this athlete famous for?
_____

_____

3. When did Kareem reach the height of 5 feet 4 inches?
_____

_____

4. Where did Kareem go to college?

5. Why did Kareem grow so tall?
_____

_____

6. How did Kareem make his living?
_____

_____

Name: _____

Comprehension: Christopher Columbus

What do you know about Christopher Columbus? He was a famous sailor and explorer. Columbus was 41 years old when he sailed from southern Spain on August 3, 1492, with three boats. On them was a crew of 90 men. It was 33 days later that he landed on Watling Island in the Bahamas. The Bahamas are islands located in the West Indies. The West Indies are a large group of islands between North America and South America.

Directions: Answer these questions about Christopher Columbus.

1. How old was Columbus when
   he set sail from southern Spain?

   _____

   _____

2. How many boats did he take?

   _____

   _____

3. How many men were with him?

   _____

4. How long did it take him to
   reach land?

   _____

   _____

5. Where did Columbus land?

   _____

   _____

   _____

Name: _____

Columbus The Explorer

Columbus was an explorer. He wanted to find out what the rest of the world looked like. He also wanted to make money! He would sail to distant islands and trade with the people there. He would buy their silks, spices and gold. Then he would sell these things in Spain. In Spain, people would pay high prices for them. Columbus got the Queen of Spain to approve his plan. She would pay for his ships and his crew. He would keep 10 percent of the value of the goods he brought back. She would take the rest. Columbus and the Queen had a business deal.

Directions: Answer these questions about Columbus.

1. Which is correct?

   Columbus and the Queen of Spain were friends.

   Columbus and the Queen of Spain were business partners.

2. Tell 2 reasons Columbus was an explorer.

   1) _____

   _____

   2) _____

   _____

3. What was Columbus' business deal with the Queen of Spain?

1) Columbus would get

_____

_____

2) In return for paying his expenses, the Queen would get

_____

_____

Comprehension: Robin Hood

Long ago in England there lived a man named Robin Hood. Robin lived with a group of other men in the woods. The woods were called Sherwood Forest. Robin Hood was a thief–a different kind of thief. He stole from the rich and gave what he stole to the poor. Poor people did not need to worry about going into Sherwood Forest. In fact, Robin Hood often gave them money. Rich people were told to beware. Robin and his men would rob the rich people. If you were rich, would you stay out of Sherwood Forest?

Directions: Answer these questions about Robin Hood.

1. What was the name of the woods where Robin Hood lived?

_____

_____

2. What did Robin Hood do for a living?

_____

_____

3. What was different about Robin Hood?

_____

_____

4. Did poor people worry about
   going into Sherwood Forest?

5. Do you think rich people worried
   about going into Sherwood Forest?

Name: _____

The King Meets Robin Hood

Everyone in England knew about Robin Hood. The king was mad! He did not want a thief to be a hero. He sent his men to Sherwood Forest to catch Robin Hood. But they could not catch him. Robin Hood outsmarted the king's men every time!

One day Robin Hood sent a message to the king. The message said, "Come with five brave men. We will see who is stronger." The king decided to fool Robin Hood. He wanted to see if what people said about Robin Hood was true. The king dressed as a monk. A monk is a poor man who serves God. Then he went to Sherwood Forest to see Robin Hood.

Directions: Answer these questions about the king and his meeting with Robin Hood.

1. If the stories about Robin Hood were true, what happened when the king met Robin Hood?

    Robin Hood robbed the king and took all his money.

    Robin Hood helped the king because he thought he was a poor man.

2. Why didn't the king want Robin Hood to know who he was?

    Because he was afraid of Robin Hood.

    Because he wanted to find out what Robin Hood was really like.

3. Why couldn't the king's men find Robin Hood?

    Because Robin Hood outsmarted them.

    Because they didn't look in Sherwood Forest.

Review

The king liked Robin Hood. He said, "Here is a man who likes a good joke." He told Robin Hood who he really was. Robin Hood was not mad. He laughed and laughed. The king invited Robin Hood to come and live in the castle. The castle was 20 miles away. Robin had to walk south, cross a river and make two left turns to get there. He stayed inside the castle grounds for a year and a day.

Then Robin grew restless and asked the king for permission to leave. The king did not want him to go. He said Robin Hood could visit Sherwood Forest for only one week. Robin said he missed his men and would not promise to return. The king knew Robin Hood never broke his promises.

Directions: Answer these questions about Robin Hood and the king.

1. Do you think Robin Hood returned to the castle? _____
   Give a reason for your answer.

   _____

   _____

2. Why do you think Robin Hood laughed when the king told him
the truth?

   _____

   _____

3. Give directions from Sherwood Forest to the king's castle.

   _____

   _____

4. The main idea is:

   Robin Hood liked the king, but he missed his life in Sherwood Forest.

   Robin Hood thought the castle was boring.

Name: _____

Grow A Pineapple Plant

You can grow a pineapple plant at home. Here's how: Have a grown-up use a large sharp knife to slice off the very "tip top" of a pineapple. Fill a five-inch round pot with potting soil. (You can get this dark soil at a garden store.) Put the top of the pineapple in the soil.

Do not bury the plant too deep. Let most of the top show. Do not give your plant too much water! Pour on a little water when you plant it. Then wait until the soil feels dry to water it again. Soon it will grow roots

Directions: Answer these questions about growing pineapple plants.

1. Where can you get potting soil?

_____

_____

_____

2. What is the first step for growing a pineapple plant?

_____

_____

_____

3. What is the second step?

_____

_____

_____

4. Be careful about these things when growing pineapple plants.

1) Do not do this: _____

_____

2) Do not do this: _____

_____

19

Name: _____

Morning Glory

Have you ever seen a morning glory? They begin to bloom in mid-May. Morning glory flowers grow on vines. They trail over the ground. Sometimes the vines twine over other plants. They will grow over walls and fences. The vines on morning glory plants can grow to be 10 feet long! Morning glory flowers are bell-shaped. The flowers are white or pink. There are more than 200 different kinds of morning glory flowers!

Directions: Answer these questions about the morning glory flower.

1. When do morning glories begin to bloom?

_____

_____

_____

2. Morning glories grow on   stems

                                                vines

3. What shape are morning glory flowers?

4. How many different kinds of morning glory flowers are there?

Name: _____

Morning Glory

Directions: Re-read the story about morning glories. Then work the puzzle.

Across
1. Morning glories grow on these.
5. Morning glories sometimes twine over these.
6. Morning glories trail over this.

Down
2. Morning glory flowers are bell-_____.
3. Morning glory flowers can be pink or _____ .
4. This is what morning glories do in mid-May.

21

How Plants Get Food

Every living thing needs food. Did you ever wonder how plants get food? They do not sit down and eat a bowl of soup! Plants get their food from the soil and from water. To see how, cut off some stalks of celery. Put the stalks in a clear glass. Fill the glass half full of water. Add a few drops of red food coloring to the water. Leave it overnight. The next day you will see that parts of the celery have turned red! The red lines show how the celery "sucked up" water. Do you see how plants get their food?

Directions: Answer these questions about how plants get their food.

1. Name two places plants get their food.

   _____   _____

   1) _____   2) _____

   _____

2. Complete the 4 steps for using celery to see how plants get food.

   1) Cut off some stalks of

   2) Put the stalks in

   3) Fill the glass

   4) Add a few drops of

3. What do the red lines in the celery show?

   _____

   _____

   _____

Fig Marigold

Fig marigolds are beautiful! The flowers stay closed unless the light is bright. These flowers also are called by another name. The other name is "mid-day flower." Mid-day flowers have leaves that are very long. The leaves are as long as your finger! There is something else unusual about mid-day flowers. They change color. When the flowers bloom, they are light yellow. After two or three days, they turn pink. Mid-day flowers grow in California and in South America where it is hot. They do not grow in other parts of the United States.

Directions: Answer these questions about the fig marigold.

1. Why do you think fig marigolds are also called mid-day flowers?

_____

_____

_____

2. How long are the leaves of the mid-day flower?

_____

_____

_____

3. Why do you think mid-day flowers do not grow all over the United States?

_____

_____

_____

Name: _____

Rain Forests

The soil in rain forests is very dark and rich. The trees and plants that grow there are very green. People who have seen one say a rain forest is "the greenest place on earth." Why? Because it rains a lot. With so much rain, the plants stay very green. The earth stays very wet. Rain forests cover only six percent of the earth. But they are home to 66 percent of all the different kinds of plants and animals on earth! Today, rain forests are threatened by such things as acid rain from factory smoke emissions around the world and from farm expansion. Farmers living near rain forests cut down many trees each year to clear the land for farming. I wish I could see a rain forest. Do you?

Directions: Answer these question about rain forests.

1. What do the plants and trees in a rain forest look like?

_____

_____

_____

2. What is the soil like in a rain forest?

_____

_____

_____

3. How much of the earth is covered by rain forests?

_____

_____

_____

4. What percentage of the earth's plants and animals live there?

_____

_____

_____

Name: _____

A Lizard Of The Rain Forest

Many strange animals live in the rain forest. One kind of strange animal is a very large lizard. The lizard grows as large as a dog! It has scales on it's skin. It has a very wide mouth. It has spikes sticking up on top of it's head. It looks very scary. But don't be afraid! This lizard eats mostly weeds. The lizard does not look very tasty. But other animals think it tastes good. Snakes eat these lizards. So do certain birds. Some people in the rain forest eat them, too! Would you like to eat a lizard for lunch?

Directions: Answer these questions about the rain forest lizard.

1. What is the size of this rain forest lizard?

_____

_____

2. Where do its scales grow?

_____

_____

3. Which kind of food does the lizard eat?

_____

_____

4. Who likes to eat these lizards?

_____

_____

5. Would you like to see this lizard?

_____

_____

Name: _____

Review

You can grow many kinds of flowers in a garden. Here are the names of some: trumpet vine, pitcher plant and bird-of-paradise. The flowers that grow on these plants form seeds. The seeds can be used to grow new plants. The bird-of-paradise looks as if it has wings! The pitcher plant is very strange. It eats insects! The trumpet vine grows very long. It trails around fences and other plants. These plants are very different. Together, they make a pretty flower garden.

Directions: Answer these questions about flower gardens.

1. What do you think a pitcher plant looks like?

_____

_____

2. What do you think a trumpet vine looks like?

_____

_____

3. Name two of the three plants that grow seeds in their flowers.

1) _____   2)_____

4. What can the seeds be used for?

_____

_____

5. What could you plant in a garden to get rid of insects?

_____

_____

Name: _____

Hawks

Hawks are birds of prey. They "prey upon" other birds and animals. This means they kill other animals and eat them. The hawk has long pointed wings. It uses them to soar in the air when it looks for prey. It looks at the ground while it soars. When it sees an animal or bird to eat, the hawk swoops down. It grabs the animal in its claws. Then it carries it off and eats it. The hawk eats sick birds, rats, ground squirrels and other pests.

Directions: Answer these questions about hawks.

1. The main idea is:

   Hawks are mean because they swoop down from the sky and eat animals and birds.

   Hawks are helpful because they eat sick birds, rats, ground squirrels and other pests.

2. What kind of wings does a hawk have?

   _____

   _____

3. How does the hawk pick up its prey?

   _____

   _____

4. What does "prey upon" mean?

   _____

   _____

   _____

Name: _____

Birds' Homing Instinct

What is instinct? (Say it this way: in-stinkt.) Instinct is knowing how to do something without being told how. Animals have instincts. Birds have an amazing instinct. It is called the "homing instinct." The homing instinct is the birds' inner urge to find their way somewhere. When birds fly south in the winter, how do they know where to go? How do they know how to get there? When they return in the spring, what makes them return to the same place they left? It is the birds' homing instinct. People do not have a homing instinct. That is why they so often get lost!

Directions: Answer these questions about birds' homing instinct.

1. What word means knowing how to do something without being told?

_____

_____

_____

2. What is the birds' inner urge to find their way somewhere called?

_____

_____

_____

3. Which direction do birds fly in the winter?

_____

_____

_____

4. Do people have a homing instinct?

_____

_____

Name: _____

Puzzling Out the Homing Instinct

Directions: Re-read the story about birds' homing instinct. Then work the puzzle.

Across

3. Knowing how to do something without being told.
4. This is when birds return from the south.
6. They have no homing instinct, so people get _____.

Down

1. Birds fly south at this time.
2. They have a homing instinct.
5. They do not have a homing instinct.

Comprehension: Pet Crickets

Did you know that some people keep crickets as pets? These people always keep two crickets together. That way, the crickets do not get lonely! The crickets are kept in a flower pot filled with dirt. The dirt helps the crickets feel at home. They are used to being outside. Over the flower pot is a covering that lets air inside. It also keeps the crickets in! Some people use a small net. Other people use cheesecloth. They make sure there is room under the covering for the crickets to hop! Pet crickets like bread and lettuce. They also like raw hamburger meat. Would you like to have a pet cricket?

Directions: Answer these questions about crickets.

1. Where do pet crickets live?

_____

_____

_____

2. Why should you put dirt with the crickets?

_____

_____

_____

3. What is put over the flowerpot?

_____

_____

_____

4. Tell 3 things pet crickets like to eat.

1) _____ 2) _____ 3) _____

Name: _____

More About Crickets

Directions: Read more about crickets. Then work the puzzle.

Only the male cricket can "sing." He "sings" by moving his right wing quickly over his left. It is sort of like playing a violin. The cricket's song is the first insect song we hear in the spring. It is the last insect song we hear in the fall. Crickets do not sing in the winter.

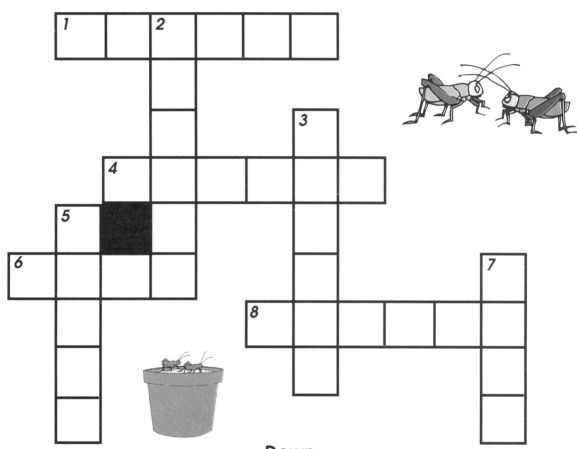

Across

1. Crickets are a kind of _____.
6. The cricket makes his song with his _____.
4. The movements for making a cricket song are like playing a _____.
8. This cricket cannot sing.

Down

2. The cricket's song is the first insect's song we hear in the _____.
3. Crickets do not sing during this season.
5. To sing, the cricket moves this wing over his left wing.
7. To sing, the cricket moves the right wing over this wing.

Name: _____

Wouldn't It Be Strange?

Directions: Read the silly poem about what the animals say. Then answer the questions.

Wouldn't it be strange?
Wouldn't you say "Wow!"
If the dog said "moo"
And the cow said "bow-wow,"
And the cat flew and sang
And the bird said "meow."
Wouldn't it be strange?
Wouldn't you say "Wow!"

1. What strange things would the cat do?

_____

_____

_____

2. What strange thing would the bird do?

_____

_____

_____

3. What strange thing would the cow do?

_____

_____

_____

4. What strange thing would the dog do?

_____

_____

_____

Name: _____

A Pussy Willow Poem

Directions: Read the poem about the pussy willow plant. Then answer the questions.

I have a little pussy
Her coat is silver gray
She's in a great wide meadow,
She never runs away.
She'll always be a pussy
She'll never be a cat.
'Cause she's a pussy willow!
What do you think of that?

1. Why does a pussy willow never run away?

_____

_____

_____

2. Why will this pussy never grow to be a cat?

_____

_____

_____

_____

_____

3. Really, what is the "coat of silver gray?"

_____

_____

_____

33

Name: _____

Review

Heather is a beautiful word for a beautiful plant. Some girls are also named Heather. Heather grows high in the mountains of the western United States. It needs very wet ground to grow in. In the high mountains, snow keeps the ground wet enough for heather. It may be as small as 4 inches high. It may grow as high as 12 inches tall. The flowers that grow on heather are a light pinkish-red color. The flowers bloom in June, July and August. Heather is a wild flower. It is one of about 250,000 flowering plants. Have you ever seen a heather plant?

Directions: Answer these questions about heather.

1. Why are some girls named Heather?

_____

_____

2. Where in the United States does heather grow?

_____

_____

3. The main idea is:

Heather is a wild flower that grows in the mountains.

Heather is one of 250,000 different kinds of plants.

4. Complete the directions on where in the U.S. to find heather.

1) Wait until these months to look for heather: _____

_____

_____

2) Go to the _____

_____

_____

3) Look for ground that is _____

_____

Name: _____

Our Solar System

There are 9 planets in our solar system. All of them circle the sun. The planet closest to the sun is named Mercury. The Greeks said Mercury was the messenger of the gods. The second planet from the sun is named Venus. Venus shines the brightest. Venus was the Greek goddess of beauty. Earth is the third planet from the sun. It is about the same size as Venus. After Earth is Mars, which is named after the Greek god of War. The other five planets are Jupiter, Saturn, Uranus, Neptune and Pluto. They, too, are named after Greek gods.

Directions: Answer these questions about our solar system.

1. How many planets are in our solar system?

2. What do the planets circle?

3. What are the planets named after?

4. Which planet is closest to the sun?

5. Which planet is about the same size as Earth?

6. Which planet comes after Earth in the solar system?

Name: _____

Mercury

In 1974, for the first time time a U.S. spacecraft passed within 400 miles of the planet Mercury. The name of the spacecraft was Mariner 10. There were no people on the spacecraft. But there were cameras that could take clear pictures from a long distance. What the pictures showed was interesting. They showed that Mercury's surface was a lot like the surface of the moon. The surface of Mercury is filled with huge holes called craters. A layer of fine dust covers Mercury. This, too, is like the dust on the moon. There is no life on either Mercury or the moon.

Directions: Answer these questions about Mercury.

1. What was the name of the spacecraft that went near Mercury?

_____

_____

2. What was on the spacecraft?

_____

_____

3. Tell two ways that Mercury is like the moon.

1) _____

_____

2) _____

_____

4. Is there life on Mercury?

_____

_____

Name: _____

Venus

For many years, no one knew much about Venus. When people looked through telescopes, they could not see past Venus' clouds. Long ago, people thought the clouds covered living things. Spacecraft radar has shown this is not true. Venus is too hot for life to exist. The temperature on Venus is about 900 degrees! Remember how hot you were the last time it was 90 degrees? Now imagine it being 10 times hotter. Nothing could exist in that heat. It is also very dry on Venus. For life to exist, water must be present. Because of the heat and dryness, we know there are no people, plants or other life on Venus.

Directions: Answer these questions about Venus.

1. The main idea is:

    We cannot see past Venus' clouds to know what the planet is like.

    Spacecraft radar show it is too hot and dry for life to exist on Venus.

2. What is the temperature on Venus? _____

3. This temperature is how many times hotter than a hot day on Earth?

    6 times hotter

    10 times hotter

4. In the past, why did people think life might exist on Venus?

_____

_____

Name: _____

Mars

The U.S. has sent spacecraft to Mars since 1964. There have been many un-manned trips to Mars. ("Unmanned" means there were no people on the spacecraft.) That's why scientists know a lot about this planet. Mars has low temperatures. There is no water on Mars. There is a gas called water vapor. There is also ice on Mars. Scientists have also learned that there is fog on Mars in the early morning! Do you remember when you last saw fog here on Earth? Scientists say the fog on Mars looks the same. As on earth, the fog occurs in low-lying areas of the ground.

Another interesting thing about Mars is that it is very windy. The wind blows up many dust storms on this planet. A spacecraft called Mariner 9 was the first to take picture of dust storms. Later, the unmanned Viking spacecraft landed on the surface of Mars.

Directions: Answer these questions about Mars.

1. On Mars, it is   cold

   hot

2. When there are no people
   on a spacecraft, it is

3. Mars and the Earth both have
   this in the early morning in
   low-lying areas.

4. These are caused by all
   the wind on Mars.

5. This spacecraft took pictures
   of dust storms on Mars.

Name: _____

Mars

Directions: Re-read the story about Mars. Then work the puzzle.

Across

1. This spacecraft landed on the surface of Mars.
3. These travel through the solar system.
5. Is it hot on Mars?
6. The wind on Mars blows up dust _____.

Down

1. There is no water on Mars. There is water _____.
2. This spacecraft took the first pictures of Mars' dust storms.
4. This occurs on Earth and on Mars in the early morning.

Name: _____

The Rings Of Saturn

Have you looked at Saturn through a strong telescope? If you have, you know it has rings. Saturn is the most beautiful planet to see! It is bright yellow. It is circled by four rings. Two bright rings are on the outside of the circle. Two dark rings are on the inside. The rings of Saturn are made of billions of tiny bits of rocks. The rocks travel around the planet in a swarm. They keep their ring shape as the planet travels around the sun. These rings shine brightly. So does the planet Saturn. Both reflect the rays of the sun. The sun is 885 million miles away from Saturn. It takes Saturn 29 and 1/2 years to travel around the sun!

Directions: Answer these questions about Saturn.

1. How many rings does Saturn have?

2. Where are Saturn's dark rings?

3. Where are Saturn's bright rings?

4. What are Saturn's rings made of?

5. What causes Saturn and its rings to shine?

6. How far away from the sun is Saturn?

Name: _____

Pluto

Pluto is the ninth planet in our solar system. It is 3,700 million miles from the sun. It cannot be seen from earth without a telescope. Maybe that is why it was named Pluto. Pluto was the Greek god of the dark underworld. For years, scientists suspected there was a ninth planet. But it was not until 1930 that a young scientist proved Pluto existed. His name was Clyde Tombaugh. He compared pictures taken at different times of the sky near Pluto. He noticed one big "star" was in a different place in different pictures. He realized it was not a star. It was a planet moving around the sun.

Directions: Answer these questions about Pluto.

1. Who discovered Pluto?

2. When did he discover Pluto?

3. Why was the new planet named Pluto?

4. How was Pluto discovered?

5. What is Pluto's distance from the sun?

Name: _____

Review

Our moon is not the only moon in the solar system. Some other planets have moons also. Saturn has 10 moons! Our moon is the Earth's closest neighbor in the solar system. Sometimes our moon is 225,727 miles away. Other times, it is 252,002 miles away. Why? Because the moon revolves around the earth. It does not go around the earth in a perfect circle. So, sometimes its path takes it further away from the earth.

When our astronauts visited the moon, here is what they found: dusty plains, high mountains and huge craters. There is no air or water on the moon. That is why life cannot exist there. The astronauts had to wear space suits to protect their skin from the bright sun. They had to take their own air to breathe. They had to take their own food and water. The moon was an interesting place to visit. But would you want to live there?

Directions: Answer these questions about our moon.

1. The main idea is:

   The moon travels around the Earth and the astronauts visited the moon.

   Astronauts found that the moon — Earth's closest neighbor — has no air or water and cannot support life.

2. Tell 3 things our astronauts found on the moon.

1) _____ 2) _____ 3) _____

3. Make a list of what to take on a trip to the moon.

_____

_____

_____

Name: _____

Your Amazing Body

Directions: Read about the human body. Then work the puzzle.

Your body is like an amazing machine. Every minute your heart pumps six quarts of blood. Your brain sends thousands of messages to the other parts of your body. The messages travel along the nerves at more than 100 miles an hour! Your lungs fill with air. Your ears hear sounds. Your eyes see pictures. And you thought you were just sitting here reading! Your body is always very busy, even when you sleep.

Across
2. Your body is an amazing _____.
4. Even when you sleep, your body is always _____.
5. You hear with these.
6. This is what you hear.

Down
1. Your eyes see these.
2. Your brain sends thousands of these to other parts of the body.
3. These fill with air.

Name: _____

Your Heart

Make your hand into a fist. Now look at it. That is about the size of your heart! Your heart is a strong pump. It works all the time. Right now, it is beating about 90 times a minute. When you run, it beats about 150 times a minute.

Inside, your heart has four spaces. The two spaces on the top are called atria. This is where blood is pumped into the heart. The two spaces on the bottom are called ventricles. This is where blood is pumped out of the heart. The blood is pumped to every part of your body. How? Open and close your fist. See how it tightens and loosens? The heart muscle tightens and loosens, too. This is how it pumps blood.

Directions: Answer these questions about your heart.

1. How often does your heart work?

_____

_____

2. How fast does it beat when you are sitting?

_____

_____

3. How fast does it beat when you are running?

_____

_____

4. How many spaces are
   inside your heart?

5. What are the heart's
   upper spaces called?

Name: _____

Your Bones

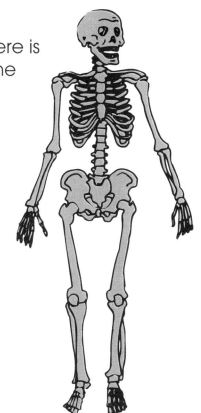

Are you scared by skeletons? You shouldn't be. There is a skeleton inside you! The skeleton is made up of all the bones in your body. These 206 bones give you your shape. They also protect your heart and everything else inside. Your bones come in many sizes. Some are short. Some are long. Some are rounded. Some are very tiny. The outside of your bones looks solid. Inside, they are filled with something soft. It is called marrow, and it is what keeps your bones alive. Red blood cells and most white blood cells are made here. These cells help to feed the body and fight disease.

Directions: Answer these questions about your bones.

1. Do you think your leg bone is short, long or rounded? _____

2. Do you think the bones in your head are short, long or rounded? _____

3. What is the size of the bones in your fingers? _____

4. What is the "something soft" inside your bones? _____

5. How many bones are in your skeleton? _____

Name: _____

Your Muscles

Can you make a fist? You could not do this without muscles. You need muscles to make your body move. You have muscles everywhere. There are muscles in your legs. There are even muscles in your tongue!

Remember, your heart is a muscle. It is called an "involuntary muscle" because it works without help from you. Your stomach muscles are also involuntary. You don't need to tell your stomach to digest food. Other muscles are called "voluntary muscles." You must tell these muscles to move. Most voluntary muscles are hooked to bones. When the muscles squeeze, they cause the bone to move. Without your muscles, you would be nothing but a "bag of bones!"

Directions: Answer these questions about your muscles.

1. What are involuntary muscles?

_____

_____

_____

2. What are voluntary muscles?

_____

_____

_____

3. These muscles are usually hooked to bones: involuntary muscles

voluntary muscles

4. What causes the bones to move?

_____

_____

_____

Name: _____

More About Your Muscles

Directions: Read more about your muscles. Then work the puzzle.

Did you know your muscles have names? No, their names are not Jason or Andrea! Their names have to do with their jobs. The muscles that pull your forearms down are called triceps. "Tri" means three. The triceps have three parts of muscle working together. The muscles that pull your forearms up are called biceps. "Bi" means two. The biceps have two parts of muscle working together. Each set of muscles has a certain job to do. Muscles in the front of the foot pull your toes up. Muscles on the back of the thighs bend your knees. Aren't you glad you have muscles?

Across

2. Each set of muscles has a certain ____ to do.
4. These muscles pull your forearms down.
5. Muscles in back of the thighs bend these.

Down

1. Without these, you would be a "bag of bones."
3. These muscles pull your forearms up.
4. Muscles on the front of your foot pull these up.

Name: _____

Your Hands

Wiggle your fingers. That was easy, wasn't it? Now clap your hands. Good job! But it wasn't as easy as you think! Each of your hands has 27 bones. Eight of the 27 bones are in your wrist. There are five bones in each of your palms. Your hands have many muscles, too. It took 30 muscles to wiggle your fingers. When you use your hands, the bones and muscles work together. Remember this the next time you cut your meat. You will use your wrist bones and muscles. You will use your finger bones and muscles. Cutting your meat seems easy. It is — thanks to your muscles and bones!

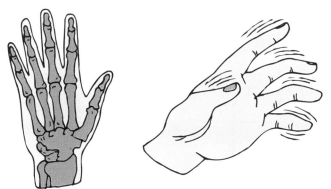

Directions: Answer these questions about your hands.

1. How many bones are in each wrist?

2. How many bones are in each of your hands?

3. How many muscles does it take to wiggle your fingers?

4. How many bones are in each of your palms?

5. Add together the palm bones and the wrist bones. Subtract from the total number of bones in the hand. How many bones are left?

Name: _____

Your Lungs

Imagine millions of teeny-tiny balloons joined together. That is what your lungs are like. When you breathe, the air goes to your two lungs. One is located on each side of your chest. The heart is located between the two lungs. The lungs are soft, spongy and delicate. That is why there are bones around the lungs. These bones are called the rib cage. The rib cage protects the lungs so they can do their job. The lungs bring oxygen into the body. (Say it this way: ox-ee-gin.) They also take a waste out of the body. This waste is called carbon dioxide. We could not live without our lungs!

Directions: Answer these questions about your lungs.

1. The main idea is:

   The lungs are spongy and located in the chest. They are like small balloons.

   The lungs bring in oxygen and take out carbon dioxide. We could not live without our lungs.

2. What is the name of the bones around our lungs?

   _____

   _____

   _____

3. What is located between the lungs?

   _____

4. What goes into your lungs when you breathe?

   _____

   _____

5. Why are there bones around our lungs?

   _____

   _____

   _____

Name: _____

Review

When you are grown, your brain will weigh only three pounds. But what an important three pounds! Billions of brain cells are packed into your brain. The cells make up the three areas of the brain. One part does your thinking and feeling. Another part of the brain helps you move your body. It also helps you keep your balance. A third part of the brain keeps you alive! It keeps your heart beating and your lungs working so you don't have to think about these things. This part of your brain is called the medulla. (Say it this way: ma-dool-la.) As long as you are alive, the medulla never rests.

Directions: Answer these questions about your brain.

1. What do you think would happen if the medulla stopped working?

_____

_____

2. What do you think would happen if something happened to the part of your brain that helps you move your body?

_____

_____

3. The main idea is:

The brain has lots of cells. Three billion cells are packed in the brain.

The brain has three areas. Each area has a very important job to do.

4. What directions does the medulla give the heart and lungs?

_____

_____

Name: _____

Searching For Ways To Travel

Directions: There are many ways to get from one place to another. Read the clues and fill in the blanks with your answers. Then circle the 8 things you can use for travel in the word search. The words may go up, down or sideways.

Q	O	X	A	L	B	N	S	B	E	R
Y	P	S	Z	R	K	I	D	I	M	P
W	G	P	O	A	L	B	S	K	I	S
H	E	L	I	C	O	P	T	E	R	K
A	Z	A	U	E	M	L	R	Q	K	A
I	U	N	J	T	S	M	A	S	Z	T
R	D	E	N	P	D	N	I	R	I	E
T	J	Z	G	B	W	D	N	B	U	S

1. This flies in the sky. **P** _ _ _ _

2. This moves on tracks. **T** _ _ _ _ _

3. You can drive this when you are 16. **C** _ _ _

4. Do you ride this to school? **B** _ _ _

5. You can travel down a snowy hill on these. **S** _ _ _ _

6. These have wheels and go on your feet. **S** _ _ _ _ _ _

7. These fly and are also called "choppers." **H** _ _ _ _ _ _ _ _ _ _

8. These have two wheels. Can you ride one? **B** _ _ _ _

Name: _____

The Horseless Carriage

Do you know how people traveled before cars? They rode horses! Often the horses were hooked up to wagons. Some horses were hooked up to carriages. Wagons were used to carry supplies. Carriages had covered tops. They were used to carry people. Both wagons and carriages were pulled by horses.

The first cars in the United States were invented shortly before the year 1900. These cars looked a lot like carriages. The seats were high off the ground. They had very thin wheels. The difference was they were powered by engines. Carriages were pulled by horses. Still, they looked alike. People called the first cars "horseless carriages."

Directions: Answer these questions about "horseless carriages."

1. Tell a way wagons and carriages were the same.

_____

_____

2. When were the first cars invented?

_____

_____

3. Why were they called horseless carriages?

_____

_____

4. What was the difference between a carriage and a horseless carriage?

_____

_____

Name: _____

The Horseless Carriage

Directions: Read more about the first cars. Then work the puzzle.

Can you guess how many cars there were in the United States 95 years ago? Only four! Today, nearly every family has a car. Most families have two cars. Henry Ford started the Ford Motor Company in 1903. His first cars were called the Model T. People thought cars would never be used in place of horses. Ford had to sell his cars through department stores! Soon, cars became "the thing." By 1920, there were 200 different U.S. companies making cars!

Across

2. He began making cars in 1903.
4. At first, cars were sold in department _____.
5. By 1920, there were 200 different companies making these.

Down

1. Henry Ford's first car was a _____.
2. At first, people thought cars would never replace ____.
3. Ford's company was called the Ford _____ Company.

A Giant Snowblower

A snowblower is used to blow snow off sidewalks and driveways. It is faster than using a shovel. It is also easier! Airports use snowblowers, too. They use them to clear the runways that planes use. Many airports use a giant snowblower. It is a type of truck. This snowblower weighs 30,000 pounds! It can blow 100,000 pounds of snow every minute. It cuts through the snow with huge blades. The blades are over six feet tall.

Directions: Answer these questions about the big trucks.

1. Why do people use snowblowers instead of shovels?

_____

_____

2. What do airports use snowblowers for?

_____

_____

3. How much do some airport snowblowers weigh?

_____

_____

4. How much snow can it blow every minute?

_____

_____

5. What does the snowblower use to cut through snow?

_____

_____

Name: _____

Early Trucks

What would we do without trucks? Your family may not own a truck. But everyone depends on trucks. Trucks bring our food to stores. Trucks deliver our furniture. Trucks carry our new clothes to shopping centers. The goods of the world move on trucks.

Trucks are harder to make than cars. They must be sturdy. They carry heavy loads. They cannot break down. The first trucks were on the road in 1900. Like trains, they were powered by steam engines. They did not use gasoline. The first trucks did not have heavy wheels. Their engines broke down. Trucks changed when the U.S. entered World War I in 1917. Big, heavy tires were put on trucks. Gasoline engines were used. Trucks used in war had to be sturdy. Lives were at stake!

Directions: Answer these questions about the first trucks.

1. What powered the first trucks?

_____

2. When did early trucks begin using gasoline engines?

_____

_____

3. How do trucks serve us?

_____

_____

4. Why did trucks used in war have to be sturdy?

_____

_____

Name: _____

The First Trains

Trains have been around much longer than cars or trucks. The first train used by America was made in England. It was brought to the U.S. in 1829. Because it was light green, it was nicknamed "the Grasshopper." Unlike a real grasshopper, this train was not fast. It only went 10 miles an hour.

That same year, another train was built by an American. Compared to the Grasshopper, the American train was fast. It went 30 miles an hour. People were amazed. This train was called the Rocket. Can you guess why?

Directions: Answer these questions about trains.

1. Where was the first train made that was used in the U.S.?

2. What did people call this train?

3. How fast did it travel?

4. What year did the Grasshopper arrive on the U.S.?

5. What American train was built that same year?

6. Why did the American train get its name?

Name: _____

The First Trains

Directions: Re-read the story of the first trains. Read the clues and fill in the blanks below with your answer. Now, find and circle these words in the word search.

```
Q  T  H  I  R  T  Y  S  B  E  R
G  R  A  S  S  H  O  P  P  E  R
R  A  P  O  A  L  B  S  K  I  O
E  I  L  I  M  O  P  T  E  R  C
E  N  G  L  A  N  D  R  Q  K  K
N  U  N  J  Z  S  M  A  S  Z  E
R  D  A  M  E  R  I  C  A  N  T
T  J  Z  G  D  W  D  N  B  U  S
```

1. This train was built by an American. **R** __ __ __ __ __

2. The first one was brought to America in 1829. **T** __ __ __ __

3. The first train brought from England. **G.** __ __ __ __ __ __ __ __ __ __ __

4. The Rocket was an **A** __ __ __ __ __ __ __ train.

5. The Grasshopper was made in **E** __ __ __ __ __ __ .

6. The Rocket went **t** __ __ __ __ __ miles an hour.

7. The train called the grasshopper was this color. **G** __ __ __ __ .

8. People were **a** __ __ __ __ __ at the speed of the American train.

Name: _____

Review

Trains are noisy! It is hard to hear around trains. That is why hand signals are used. The signals tell the engineer who drives the train many things. There is a signal to tell him to stop completely. Another signal tells him to reduce his speed. Other signals tell the engineer to proceed, apply brakes, release brakes, and back up. These six signals are very important.

During daylight, the signals are made with a white or red kerchief. At night, the signals are made with a big lantern that can be seen easily. A "signal man" moves the lantern. The arrows in the pictures show which way the lantern is moved.

| stop | reduce speed | apply brakes | release breaks | back up | proceed |

Directions: Answer these questions about hand signals for trains.

1. Why is a lantern used for hand signals at night?

_____

_____

2. Who drives the train?

3. How many hand signals does the story tell about?

_____

_____

4. Look at the pictures. Give directions for signaling the engineer to stop.

_____

_____

Name: _____

Rhinos

Rhinos are the second-largest land animal. Only elephants are bigger.

Most people think rhinos are ugly. Their full name is "rhinoceros" (rhy-noss-ur-us). There are five kinds of rhinos: square-lipped rhino, black rhino, Great Indian rhino, Sumatran rhino (say it this way: sue-ma-trahn) and Javan rhino.

Rhinos have a good sense of smell. It also helps protect them. They can smell other animals far away. They don't eat them though. Rhinos do not eat meat. They are vegetarians. (Say it this way: veg-e-tair-ee-uns.)

Directions: Answer these questions about rhinos.

1. What is the largest land animal? _____
_____
_____

2. What are the 5 kinds of rhinos? _____

1) _____ 2) _____
_____ _____

3) _____ 4) _____
_____ _____

5) _____
_____

Name: _____

Robins

Have you ever heard this old song? "Oh, the red, red robin, goes bob-bob-bobbin along!" It"s hard to not smile when you see a robin. Robins were first called "redbreasts ." If you have seen one, you know why! The fronts of their bodies are red. Robins are cheerful-looking birds.

Robins sing a sweet, mellow song. That is another reason people like robins.The female robin lays two to six eggs. She sits on them for two weeks. Then the father and the mother robin both bring food to the baby birds. Robins eat spiders, worms, insects and small seeds. Robins will also eat food scraps people put out for them.

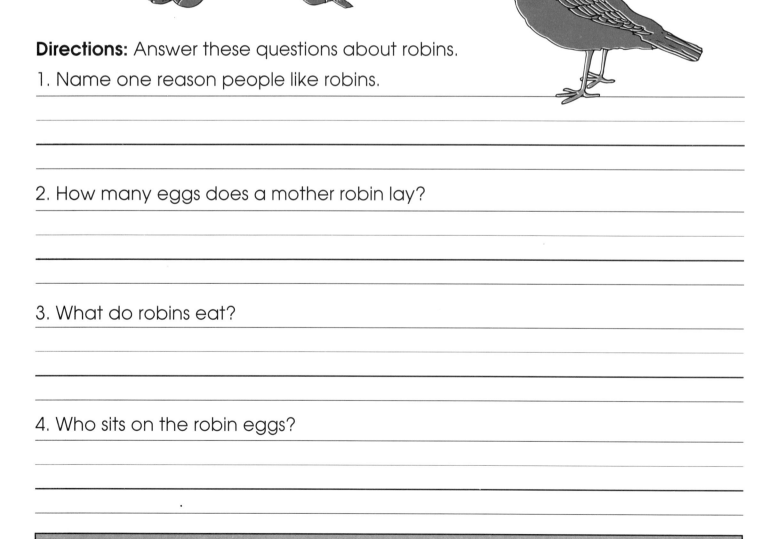

Directions: Answer these questions about robins.

1. Name one reason people like robins.

_____

_____

2. How many eggs does a mother robin lay?

_____

_____

3. What do robins eat?

_____

_____

4. Who sits on the robin eggs?

_____

_____

Name: _____

A Puzzle For The Birds

Directions: Re-read the story about robins. Then work the puzzle.

Across
1. One type of food robins eat.
3. The mother robin lays from two to six of these.
4. Robins are ____ looking birds.
5. Mother and father robin bring this to their babies.
6. Another type of food robins eat.

Down
1. The robin's ____ is sweet and mellow.
2. Robins were first called by this name.

61

Name: _____

Rodents

You are surrounded by rodents (row-dents)! There are 1,500 different kinds of rodents. One of the most common rodents is the mouse. Rats, gophers (go-furs) and beavers are rodents. So are squirrels and porcupines (pork-a-pines).

All rodents have a set of long , sharp teeth. These sharp teeth are called incisors (in-size-ors). Rodents use these teeth to eat their food. They eat mostly seeds and vegetables. There is one type of rodent some children have as a pet. No, it is not a rat! It is the guinea (ginney) pig.

Directions: Answer these questions about rodents.

1. How many kinds are rodents are there?

_____
_____
_____

2. Name 7 kinds of rodents.

1) _____ 2) _____ 3) _____

4) _____ 5) _____

6) _____ 7) _____

3. What are rodents' sharp teeth called? _____
_____
_____

4. What rodent is sometimes a pet? _____
_____

Name: _____

Sheep

Sheep like to stay close together. They do not run off. They move together in a flock. They live on sheep ranches. Some sheep grow 20 pounds of fleece each year. After it is cut off, the fleece is called wool. Cutting off the wool is called "shearing". It does not hurt the sheep to be sheared. The wool is very warm and is used to make clothing.

Female sheep are called ewes ("yous"). Some types of ewes have only one baby each year. The baby is called a lamb. Other types of ewes have two or three lambs each year.

Directions: Answer these questions about sheep.

1. Why is sheep's behavior helpful to sheep ranchers?

_____

_____

_____

2. Would you rather own the kind of sheep that has one baby each year? Or would you rather have the kind that has two or three babies?

_____

_____

_____

3. Why?

_____

_____

_____

4. When it is still on the sheep, what is wool called?

_____

5. What is a group of sheep called?

_____

Name: _____

Review

Have you ever smelled a skunk? A skunk's oder helps protect him. The smell comes from scent (sent) glands under the skunk's tail. These scent glands make a liquid (lick quid) that smells very bad. The skunk can shoot the liquid 10 feet. into the air . The skunk shoots it to protect itself.The skunk arches its back before it shoots.

There are ten types of skunks. The most common type is black. It has a white strip down its head and back. It has a black tip to its tail. Some people have skunks for pets. What do you think they have removed from the skunk first?

Directions: Answer these questions about skunks.

1. Give directions on what to do to have a skunk for a pet?

_____

_____

2. What would you do if you saw a wild skunk arch its back?

_____

_____

3. Why?

_____

_____

_____

4. How many types of skunks are there? _____

_____

Dictionary Mystery

Here are six dictionary entries.
There are pronunciations.
There are the definitions.
There are sample sentences.
The only things missing are the entry words.
Try to add the correct entry words.
Be sure to spell each entry word correctly.

rainbow
(rān´ bō)

Entry word

_____

(rōz)
A flower that grows on bushes
and vines.
The red rose smells sweet.

Entry word

_____

(foks)
A wild animal that lives in
the woods.
The fox hunts for its food.

Entry word

_____

(lāk)
A body of water that is
surrounded by land.
Let's go swimming in the lake.

Entry word

_____

(rab′it)
A small animal that has
long ears.
My rabbit can hop.

Entry word

_____

(pē an′ō)
A musical instrument that
has many keys.
I take piano lessons.

Entry word

_____

(bās′bôl′)
A game played with a bat
and a ball.
I am on a baseball team.

Understanding dictionary entries

An Opposites Poem

Read the silly poem below and then rewrite it.
Change every underlined word into an opposite.

In the beautiful land of Goop-dee-goo
   Everyone eats a sweet apple stew.
The boys walk backwards all day long
   And whisper when they sing a song.
The girls are always kind and fair.
   They have big thumbs and long green hair.
It never rains, so remember that—
   You won't need an umbrella or a hat.
Please come along here to Goop-dee-goo,
   We'll all be looking out for you.

Peggy Kaye

Rewrite the poem here.

_____

_____

_____

_____

_____

_____

_____

_____

_____

Read the new poem you made.
Which poem do you think is sillier? Circle your answer.   Poem 1   Poem 2

Using antonyms

Which Word?

The sun and its planets move through the Milky Way.
Do you know how fast the sun and planets are moving?
To find out, write the correct word in each sentence.
Look at the number next to the word you chose.
Write that number in the Number Box.
Start at the left and do not skip any spaces.
Add up all the numbers you wrote and
put the sum on the last line in the box.

Come over _____.	hear **10**	here **20**
The wind _____ all night.	blew **25**	blue **15**
I can _____ you.	see **25**	sea **10**
That mouse has a long _____.	tail **15**	tale **10**
We _____ the race!	one **15**	won **30**
Look at my _____ bike.	knew **20**	new **25**
How much does a whale _____?	weigh **20**	way **15**
Put the belt on your _____.	waste **10**	waist **15**

Number Box

_____ + _____ + _____ + _____ + _____ + _____ + _____ + _____ = _____

Complete this sentence with the sum from the Number Box.

The sun and planets travel _____ miles every second!

Using homophones in context

Word Puzzle

There are two sentences for each word that goes
in the puzzle below.
Try to think of one word that fits both sentences.
Write that word in the puzzle, one letter to a box.

Across

2. You _____ go to the show.
   My birthday is on _____ 11th.

3. I _____ a blue bird.
   I will _____ the wood.

4. Do not _____ the bus.
   My teacher is _____ Jones.

5. _____ me the book.
   Look at the clock's big _____.

8. You have dirt on your _____.
   A clock has hands and a _____.

9. I will act in a _____.
   I want to _____ baseball.

Down

1. Turn on the _____.
   The bag feels _____.

2. I know what you _____.
   Be nice! Don't be _____.

6. I will _____ the cards.
   It is a fair _____.

7. They _____ 1 hour ago.
   It is in my _____ hand.

8. The bird can _____.
   Don't let the _____ in
   the house.

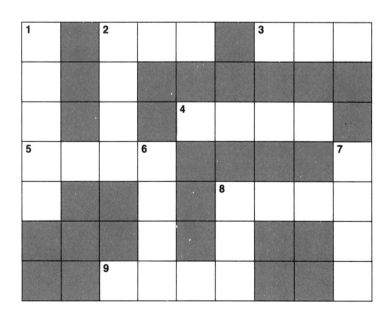

Using words with multiple meanings

What Is My Job?

Play this game with an adult.
Look at the lists of jobs below.
Pick one of them or choose any other job you want.
Do not tell your adult which one you chose.
Tell three things about the job, but do not give its name.
Here is an example.

   You come to me when you are hungry.
   I sell fruits, vegetables, and other kinds of food.
   When you finish visiting me, you go home with
   a bag full of good things to eat.
   What is my job?

If your adult can guess the job, score 1 point.
Take turns.
Play three rounds and keep score in the Score Box.

JOBS

a cook	a carpenter	a ballet dancer
a doctor	a bank teller	an animal trainer
a plumber	a fire fighter	a pet store owner
a teacher	a mail carrier	a shoe salesperson
a musician	a window washer	a newspaper reporter

Score Box	
Me	**My Adult**
Round 1	Round 1
Round 2	Round 2
Round 3	Round 3
Total	Total

Using information to make inferences

Problems, Problems

Ask an adult to work on these problems with you.

My Problems

Read this problem to yourself.

You are in a food store. You want to pay for the food, but you forgot your money at home. What do you do?

Read these three plans.
Underline the plan that tells what you would do.

1. Go home and get money.
2. Ask the storekeeper to wait for the money.
3. Phone a friend to bring money.

Now read the same problem and plans to your adult.
Circle the choice your adult picks.

Read this problem to yourself.

Your favorite TV show is on, but your TV is not working. What do you do?

Read these three plans.
Underline the plan that tells what you would do.

1. Forget the show for tonight.
2. Visit a friend and watch the show there.
3. Try to fix the TV.

Now read the same problem and plans to your adult.
Circle the choice your adult picks.

My Adult's Problem

Let your adult have a turn reading this problem and its plans with you.

You are rushing to get ready for school and juice spills on your homework. What do you do?

1. Give the teacher the homework with juice stains on it.
2. Redo the homework before school starts.
3. Leave the homework at home and tell the teacher what happened.

Now write the number of the plan that tells what you would do. _____

My adult thought I would pick plan number _____.

Pyramids

Do this with a friend.
How was a pyramid built by the Egyptians of long ago?
It was hard work, and it took many years.
Here are four different pyramid building plans.
Only one plan gives the correct order for building a pyramid.
Read each plan.
Decide which plan is in correct order.

1. The land is measured.
   The desert is cleared.
   The pointed stone is set on top.
   The stones are put in place.
   The stones are polished.

2. The desert is cleared.
   The land is measured.
   The stones are put in place.
   The pointed stone is set on top.
   The stones are polished.

3. The desert is cleared.
   The stones are put in place.
   The land is measured.
   The stones are polished.
   The pointed stone is set on top.

4. The stones are put in place.
   The pointed stone is set on top.
   The stones are polished.
   The land is measured.
   The desert is cleared.

Which plan do you think is correct?   1   2   3   4

Which plan does your friend think is correct?   1   2   3   4

Which way is correct?
Answer this upside down question, and you will find out.

——————— How many shoes are in a pair?

That is the correct plan number for pyramid building.

Air and Water

This activity is for you to do with an adult.
Read these statements together.

1. Oceans and seas take up about $\frac{2}{3}$ of the earth's surface.
2. The average person uses 168 gallons of water a day.
3. You can live for two weeks without food, two days without water, but only several minutes without air.
4. One molecule out of every 500 molecules of air you breathe has been exhaled by another person.
5. A single car produces more than a ton of harmful gases each year.

Circle the statements you think are true.　　1　　2　　3　　4　　5

Circle the statements your adult thinks are true.　　1　　2　　3　　4　　5

Now read the two paragraphs below.
Statements 1, 3, and 5 are true if everything in both paragraphs makes sense.
Statements 2 and 4 are true if everything in one paragraph makes sense but there is nonsense in the other.
All the statements are true if both paragraphs have nonsense.

1. We all need clean air to breathe, but it is hard to keep our air clean. Cars, machines, and factories all create bad gases that dirty the air. Scientists must work hard to find new ways to make our air hard to breathe. Our government has laws telling companies to keep our air as clean as possible. Working together, we can make sure that we always have clean air to breathe.

2. Water pollution is another bad problem. How can we keep our waters polluted and unsafe for fish, people, animals, and plants? Governments all over the world must act together to protect the oceans. Businesses must develop ways to protect our waterways, too. We must all help to keep the water clean.

Identifying inconsistencies

ANSWER KEY

MASTER COMPREHENSION
3

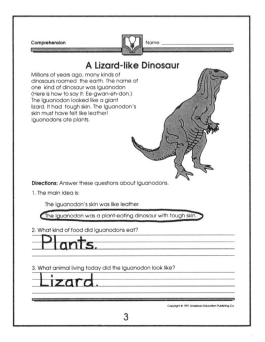

A Lizard-like Dinosaur

Millions of years ago, many kinds of dinosaurs roamed the earth. The name of one kind of dinosaur was Iguanodon (Here is how to say it: Ee-gwan-eh-don.) The Iguanodon looked like a giant lizard. It had tough skin. The Iguanodon's skin must have felt like leather! Iguanodons ate plants.

Directions: Answer these questions about Iguanodons.

1. The main idea is:

   The Iguanodon's skin was like leather.

   The Iguanodon was a plant-eating dinosaur with tough skin.

2. What kind of food did Iguanodons eat?

   Plants.

3. What animal living today did the Iguanodon look like?

   Lizard.

3

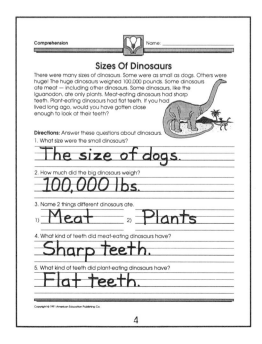

Sizes Of Dinosaurs

There were many sizes of dinosaurs. Some were as small as dogs. Others were huge! The huge dinosaurs weighed 100,000 pounds. Some dinosaurs ate meat — including other dinosaurs. Some dinosaurs, like the Iguanodon, ate only plants. Meat-eating dinosaurs had sharp teeth. Plant-eating dinosaurs had flat teeth. If you had lived long ago, would you have gotten close enough to look at their teeth?

Directions: Answer these questions about dinosaurs.

1. What size were the small dinosaurs?

   The size of dogs.

2. How much did the big dinosaurs weigh?

   100,000 lbs.

3. Name 2 things different dinosaurs ate.

   1) Meat   2) Plants

4. What kind of teeth did meat-eating dinosaurs have?

   Sharp teeth.

5. What kind of teeth did plant-eating dinosaurs have?

   Flat teeth.

4

Dining Dinosaurs

Brontosaurus dinosaurs lived in the swamps. Swamps are water areas where many plants grow. Here are the names of the other kinds of dinosaurs that lived in the swamps. The way to say their names is shown inside the ( ). Diplodocus (dip-low-dock-us), Brachiosaurus (Bracky-o-saur-us) and Cetiosaurus (Set-e-o-saur-us). These dinosaurs had small heads and small brains. They weighed 20 tons or more. They grew to be 60 feet long! These animals did not need to have sharp teeth.

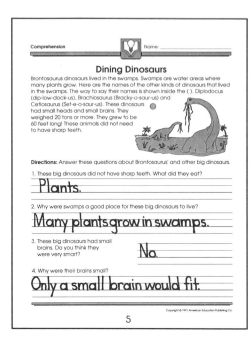

Directions: Answer these questions about Brontosaurus' and other big dinosaurs.

1. These big dinosaurs did not have sharp teeth. What did they eat?

Plants.

2. Why were swamps a good place for these big dinosaurs to live?

Many plants grow in swamps.

3. These big dinosaurs had small brains. Do you think they were very smart?

_No._

4. Why were their brains small?

Only a small brain would fit.

5

When Dinosaurs Roamed

Dinosaurs roamed the earth for 125 million years. Can you imagine that much time? About 40 years ago, some people found fossils of dinosaur tracks in Connecticut. Fossils are rocks that hold the hardened bones, eggs and footprints of animals that lived long ago. The fossil tracks showed that many dinosaurs walked together in herds. The fossils showed more than 2,000 dinosaur tracks!

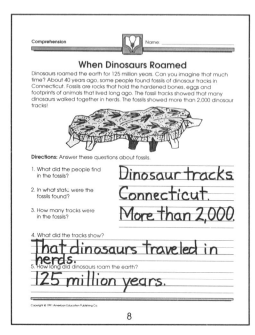

Directions: Answer these questions about fossils.

1. What did the people find in the fossils?

Dinosaur tracks

2. In what state were the fossils found?

Connecticut.

3. How many tracks were in the fossils?

More than 2,000.

4. What did the tracks show?

That dinosaurs traveled in herds.

5. How long did dinosaurs roam the earth?

125 million years.

8

Dinosaurs Were Cold-Blooded

Like snakes, dinosaurs were cold-blooded. Cold-blooded animals cannot keep themselves warm. Because of this, dinosaurs were not very active when it was cold. In the early morning, they did not move much. When the sun grew warm, the dinosaurs became active. When the sun went down in the evening, they slowed down again for the night. The sun warmed the dinosaurs and gave them the energy they needed to move about.

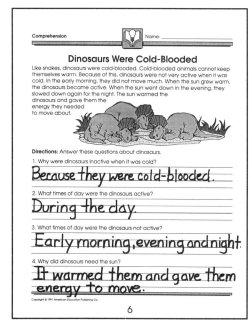

Directions: Answer these questions about dinosaurs.

1. Why were dinosaurs inactive when it was cold?

Because they were cold-blooded.

2. What times of day were the dinosaurs active?

During the day.

3. What times of day were the dinosaurs not active?

Early morning, evening and night.

4. Why did dinosaurs need the sun?

It warmed them and gave them energy to move.

6

Dinosaur Models

Some people can build models of dinosaurs. The models are fakes, of course. But they are life size and they look real! The people who build them must know the dinosaur inside and out. First they build a skeleton. Then they cover it with fake "skin." Then they paint it. Some models have motors in them. The motors can make the dinosaur's head or tail move. Have you ever seen a life-size model of a dinosaur?

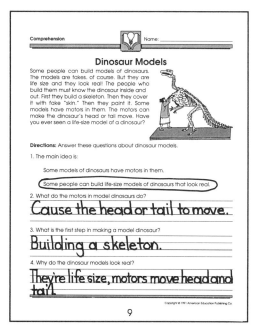

Directions: Answer these questions about dinosaur models.

1. The main idea is:

Some models of dinosaurs have motors in them.

(Some people can build life-size models of dinosaurs that look real.)

2. What do the motors in model dinosaurs do?

Cause the head or tail to move.

3. What is the first step in making a model dinosaur?

Building a skeleton.

4. Why do the dinosaur models look real?

They're life size, motors move head and tail.

9

Tyrannosaurus Rex

One of the biggest dinosaurs was Tyrannosaurus Rex. (Here is how to say his name: Ty-ran-oh-saur-us Recks.) This dinosaur walked on its two big back legs. It had two small, short front legs. From the top of his head to the tip of his tail, Tyrannosaurus measured 50 feet long. His head was 4 feet long! Are you taller than this dinosaur's head? Tyrannosaurus was a meat-eater. He had many small sharp teeth. His favorite meal was a smaller dinosaur that had a bill like a duck. This smaller dinosaur lived near water.

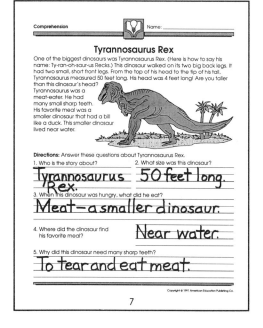

Directions: Answer these questions about Tyrannosaurus Rex.

1. Who is the story about?

Tyrannosaurus Rex.

2. What size was this dinosaur?

50 feet long.

3. When this dinosaur was hungry, what did he eat?

Meat — a smaller dinosaur.

4. Where did the dinosaur find his favorite meal?

Near water.

5. Why did this dinosaur need many sharp teeth?

To tear and eat meat.

7

Review

There are no dinosaurs alive today. They became extinct millions of years ago. This was before people lived on earth. (Say the word this way: ex-tinkt.) When animals are extinct, they are gone forever. No one know exactly why dinosaurs became extinct. Some scientists say that a disease may have killed them all. Other scientists say a huge hot rock called a comet hit the earth. The comet caused a big fire. The fire killed the dinosaurs' food. Still other scientists believe that the earth grew very cold. The dinosaurs died because they could not keep warm. Many scientists have ideas, but no one can know for sure just what happened.

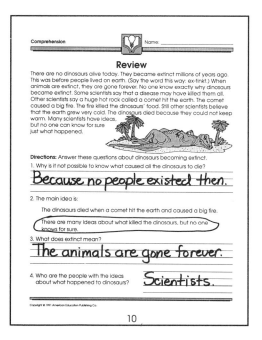

Directions: Answer these questions about dinosaurs becoming extinct.

1. Why is it not possible to know what caused all the dinosaurs to die?

Because no people existed then.

2. The main idea is:

The dinosaurs died when a comet hit the earth and caused a big fire.

(There are many ideas about what killed the dinosaurs, but no one knows for sure.)

3. What does extinct mean?

The animals are gone forever.

4. Who are the people with the ideas about what happened to dinosaurs?

Scientists.

10

Athletes' Nicknames

Directions: Read about nicknames. Then work the puzzle.

Do you have a nickname? Nicknames are the silly names people call each other. Sometimes nicknames are mean. Usually nicknames are nice. Most people do not mind if their friends make up a nice nickname for them. Many athletes have nicknames. Have you heard of a football player named "Refrigerator" Perry? He is very big! How about a basketball player named "Magic" Johnson? Can you guess why he got that nickname?

Across
2. "Refrigerator" is very _____ .
4. The silly names that people call each other.
5. "Magic" Johnson is a basketball _____ .

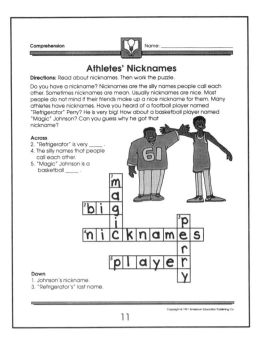

Crossword answers:
1. magic
2. big
4. nicknames
3. perry
5. player

Down
1. Johnson's nickname.
3. "Refrigerator's" last name.

11

Christopher Columbus

What do you know about Christopher Columbus? He was a famous sailor and explorer. Columbus was 41 years old when he sailed from Southern Spain on August 3, 1492 with three boats. On them was a crew of 90 men. It was 33 days later that he landed on Watling Island in the Bahamas. The Bahamas are islands located in the West Indies. The West Indies are a large group of islands between North America and South America.

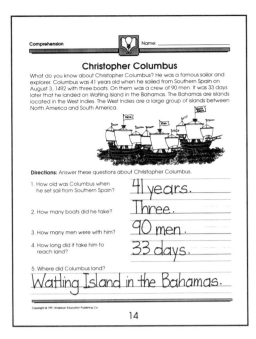

Directions: Answer these questions about Christopher Columbus.

1. How old was Columbus when he set sail from Southern Spain?   **41 years.**

2. How many boats did he take?   **Three.**

3. How many men were with him?   **90 men.**

4. How long did it take him to reach land?   **33 days.**

5. Where did Columbus land?   **Watling Island in the Bahamas.**

14

Kareem Abdul Jabar

Have you heard of a basketball star named Kareem Abdul Jabar? When he was born, Kareem's name was Lew Alcindor. He was named after his father. When he was in college, Kareem changed his religion from Christian to Muslim. That is when he took the Muslim name of Kareem Abdul Jabar.

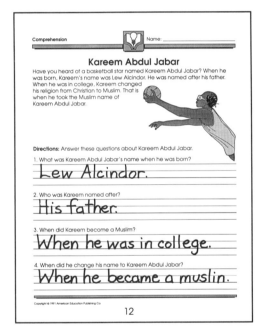

Directions: Answer these questions about Kareem Abdul Jabar.

1. What was Kareem Abdul Jabar's name when he was born?
Lew Alcindor.

2. Who was Kareem named after?
His father.

3. When did Kareem become a Muslim?
When he was in college.

4. When did he change his name to Kareem Abdul Jabar?
When he became a muslin.

12

Columbus The Explorer

Columbus was an explorer. He wanted to find out what the rest of the world looked like. He also wanted to make money! He would sail to distant islands and trade with the people there. He would buy their silks, spices and gold. Then he would sell these things in Spain. In Spain, people would pay high prices for them. Columbus got the Queen of Spain to approve his plan. She would pay for his ships and his crew. He would keep 10 percent of the value of the goods he brought back. She would take the rest. Columbus and the Queen had a business deal.

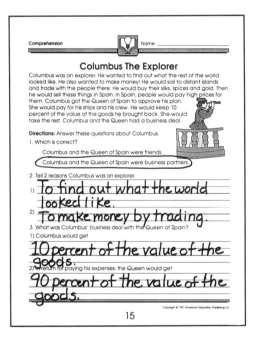

Directions: Answer these questions about Columbus.

1. Which is correct?
   Columbus and the Queen of Spain were friends.
   (Columbus and the Queen of Spain were business partners.)

2. Tell 2 reasons Columbus was an explorer.
1) **To find out what the world looked like.**
2) **To make money by trading.**

3. What was Columbus' business deal with the Queen of Spain?
1) Columbus would get **10 percent of the value of the goods.**
2) In return for paying his expenses, the Queen would get **90 percent of the value of the goods.**

15

Recognizing Details: Kareem Abdul Jabbar

Kareem Abdul Jabar grew up to be more than 7 feet tall! Kareem's father and mother were both very tall. When he was 9 years old, Kareem was already 5 feet 4 inches tall. Kareem was raised in New York City. He went to Power Memorial High School and played basketball on that team. He went to college at UCLA. He played basketball in college, too. At UCLA, Kareem's team lost only 2 games in 3 years! After college, Kareem made his living playing basketball.

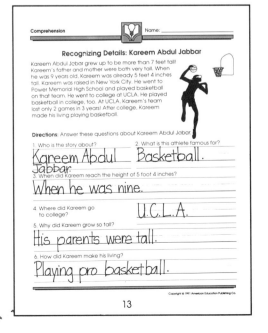

Directions: Answer these questions about Kareem Abdul Jabar.

1. Who is the story about?
Kareem Abdul Jabbar.

2. What is this athlete famous for?
Basketball.

3. When did Kareem reach the height of 5 foot 4 inches?
When he was nine.

4. Where did Kareem go to college?
U.C.L.A.

5. Why did Kareem grow so tall?
His parents were tall.

6. How did Kareem make his living?
Playing pro basketball.

13

Robin Hood

Long ago in England there lived a man named Robin Hood. Robin lived with a group of other men in the woods. The woods were called Sherwood Forest. Robin Hood was a thief — a different kind of thief. He stole from the rich and gave what he stole to the poor. Poor people did not need to worry about going into Sherwood Forest. If fact, Robin Hood often gave them money. Rich people were told to beware. Robin and his men would rob the rich people. If you were rich, would you stay out of Sherwood Forest?

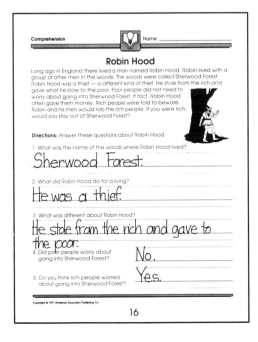

Directions: Answer these questions about Robin Hood.

1. What was the name of the woods where Robin Hood lived?
Sherwood Forest.

2. What did Robin Hood do for a living?
He was a thief.

3. What was different about Robin Hood?
He stole from the rich and gave to the poor.

4. Did poor people worry about going into Sherwood Forest?   **No.**

5. Do you think rich people worried about going into Sherwood Forest?   **Yes.**

16

The King Meets Robin Hood

Everyone in England knew about Robin Hood. The King was mad! He did not want a thief to be a hero. He sent his men to Sherwood Forest to catch Robin Hood. But they could not catch him. Robin Hood outsmarted the King's men every time!

One day Robin Hood sent a message to the King. The message said, "Come with five brave men. We will see who is stronger." The king decided to fool Robin Hood. He wanted to see if what people said about Robin Hood was true. The King dressed as a monk. A monk is a poor man who serves God. Then he went to Sherwood Forest to see Robin Hood.

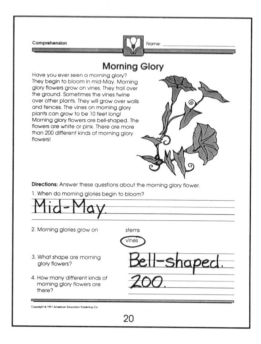

Directions: Answer these questions about the King and his meeting with Robin Hood.

1. If the stories about Robin Hood were true, what happened when the King met Robin Hood?

    Robin Hood robbed the King and took all his money.

    (Robin Hood helped the King because he thought he was a poor man.)

2. Why didn't the King want Robin Hood to know who he was?

    Because he was afraid of Robin Hood.

    (Because he wanted to find out what Robin Hood was really like.)

3. Why couldn't the King's men find Robin Hood?

    (Because Robin Hood outsmarted them.)

    Because they didn't look in Sherwood Forest.

17

Review

The King liked Robin Hood. He said, "Here is a man who likes a good joke." He told Robin Hood who he really was. Robin Hood was not mad. He laughed and laughed. The King invited Robin Hood to come and live in the castle. The castle was 20 miles away. Robin had to walk south, cross a river and make two left turns to get there. He stayed inside the castle grounds for a year and a day.

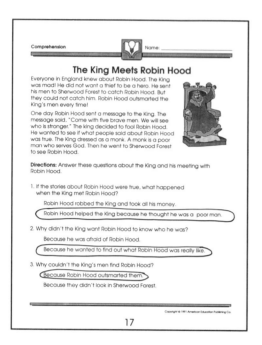

Then Robin grew restless and asked the King to leave. The King did not want him to go. He said Robin Hood could visit Sherwood Forest for only one week. Robin said he missed his men and would not promise to return. The King knew Robin Hood never broke his promises.

Directions: Answer these questions about Robin Hood and the King.

1. Do you think Robin Hood returned to the castle? **No.**
Give a reason for your answer.

Robin Hood never broke promises.

2. Why do you think Robin Hood laughed when the King told him the truth?

He enjoyed the joke the King played on him.

3. Give directions from Sherwood Forest to the King's castle.

South 20 miles, cross a river make two left turns.

4. The main idea is:

    (Robin Hood liked the King but he missed his life in Sherwood Forest.)

    Robin Hood thought the castle was boring.

18

Grow A Pineapple Plant

You can grow a pineapple plant at home. Here's how: Have a grownup use a large sharp knife to slice off the very "tip top" of a pineapple. Fill a five-inch round pot with potting soil. (You can get this dark soil at a garden store.) Put the top of the pineapple in the soil.

Do not bury the plant too deep. Let most of the top show.

Do not give your plant too much water! Pour on a little water when you plant it. Then wait until the soil feels dry to water it again. Soon it will grow roots.

Directions: Answer these questions about growing pineapple plants.

1. Where can you get potting soil?

Garden store.

2. What is the first step for growing a pineapple plant?

Slice off the "tip top".

3. What is the second step?

Fill a 5 inch round pot with soil.

4. Be careful about these things when growing pineapple plants.

1) Do not do this: **Bury the plant too deep.**

2) Do not do this: **Give it too much water.**

19

Morning Glory

Have you ever seen a morning glory? They begin to bloom in mid-May. Morning glory flowers grow on vines. They trail over the ground. Sometimes the vines twine over other plants. They will grow over walls and fences. The vines on morning glory plants can grow to be 10 feet long! Morning glory flowers are bell-shaped. The flowers are white or pink. There are more than 200 different kinds of morning glory flowers!

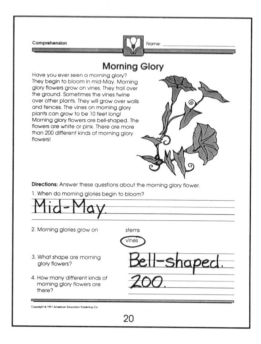

Directions: Answer these questions about the morning glory flower.

1. When do morning glories begin to bloom?

Mid-May.

2. Morning glories grow on   stems   (vines)

3. What shape are morning glory flowers?

Bell-shaped.

4. How many different kinds of morning glory flowers are there?

200.

20

Morning Glory

Directions: Re-read the story about morning glories. Then work the puzzle.

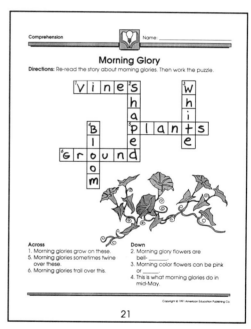

Crossword answers: VINES, SHAPED, WHITE, BLOOM, PLANTS, GROUND

Across
1. Morning glories grow on these.
5. Morning glories sometimes twine over these.
6. Morning glories trail over this.

Down
2. Morning glory flowers are bell-_____.
3. Morning color flowers can be pink or _____.
4. This is what morning glories do in mid-May.

21

How Plants Get Food

Every living thing needs food. Did you ever wonder how plants get food? They do not sit down and eat a bowl of soup! Plants get their food from the soil and from water. To see how, cut off some stalks of celery. Put the stalks in a clear glass. Fill the glass half full of water. Add a few drops of red food coloring to the water. Leave it overnight. The next day you will see that parts of the celery have turned red! The red lines show how the celery "sucked up" water. Do you see how plants get their food?

Directions: Answer these questions about how plants get their food.

1. Name two places plants get their food.

1) **Soil.**   2) **Water.**

2. Complete the 4 steps for using celery to see how plants get food.

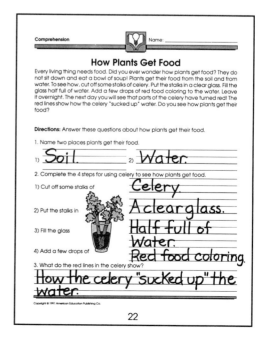

1) Cut off some stalks of   **Celery.**

2) Put the stalks in   **A clear glass.**

3) Fill the glass   **Half full of water.**

4) Add a few drops of   **Red food coloring.**

3. What do the red lines in the celery show?

How the celery "sucked up" the water.

22

Fig Marigold

Fig marigolds are beautiful! The flowers stay closed unless the light is bright. These flowers also are called by another name. The other name is "mid-day flower." Mid-day flowers have leaves that are very long. The leaves are as long as your finger! There is something else unusual about mid-day flowers. They change color. When the flowers bloom, they are light yellow. After two or three days, they turn pink. Mid-day flowers grow in California and in South America where it is hot. They do not grow in other parts of the United States.

Directions: Answer these questions about the fig marigold.

1. Why do you think Fig marigolds are also called mid-day flowers?

The flowers open mid-day.

2. How long are the leaves of the mid-day flower?

As long as your finger.

3. Why do you think mid-day flowers do not grow all over the United States?

Because it is not hot enough.

23

Review

You can grow many kinds of flowers in a garden. Here are the names of some: trumpet vine, pitcher plant and bird-of-paradise. The flowers that grow on these plants form seeds. The seeds can be used to grow new plants. The bird-of-paradise looks as if it has wings! The pitcher plant is very strange. It eats insects! The trumpet vine grows very long. It trails around fences and other plants. These plants are very different. Together, they make a pretty flower garden.

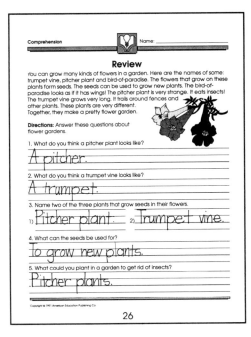

Directions: Answer these questions about flower gardens.

1. What do you think a pitcher plant looks like?

A pitcher.

2. What do you think a trumpet vine looks like?

A trumpet.

3. Name two of the three plants that grow seeds in their flowers.

1) *Pitcher plant.*   2) *Trumpet vine.*

4. What can the seeds be used for?

To grow new plants.

5. What could you plant in a garden to get rid of insects?

Pitcher plants.

26

Rain Forests

The soil in rain forests is very dark and rich. The trees and plants that grow there are very green. People who have seen one say a rain forest is "the greenest place on earth." Why? Because it rains a lot. With so much rain, the plants stay very green. The earth stays very wet. Rain forests cover only six percent of the earth. But they are home to 66 percent of all the different kinds of plants and animals on earth! Today, rain forests are threatened by such things as acid rain from factory smoke emissions around the world and from farm expansion. Farmers living near rain forests cut down many trees each year to clear the land for faming. I wish I could see a rain forest. Do you?

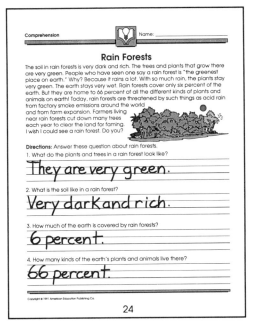

Directions: Answer these question about rain forests.

1. What do the plants and trees in a rain forest look like?

They are very green.

2. What is the soil like in a rain forest?

Very dark and rich.

3. How much of the earth is covered by rain forests?

6 percent.

4. How many kinds of the earth's plants and animals live there?

66 percent.

24

Hawks

Hawks are birds of prey. They "prey upon," other birds and animals. This means they kill other animals and eat them. The hawk has long pointed wings. It uses them to soar in the air when it looks for prey. It looks at the ground while it soars. When it sees an animal or bird to eat, the hawk swoops down. It grabs the animal in its claws. Then it carries it off and eats it. The hawk eats sick birds, rats, ground squirrels and other pests.

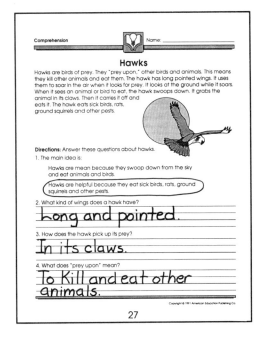

Directions: Answer these questions about hawks.

1. The main idea is:

     Hawks are mean because they swoop down from the sky and eat animals and birds.

     (Hawks are helpful because they eat sick birds, rats, ground squirrels and other pests.) ⟵ circled

2. What kind of wings does a hawk have?

Long and pointed.

3. How does the hawk pick up its prey?

In its claws.

4. What does "prey upon" mean?

To kill and eat other animals.

27

A Lizard Of The Rain Forest

Many strange animals live in the rain forest. One kind of strange animal is a very large lizard. The lizard grows as large as a dog! It has scales on its skin. It has a very wide mouth. It has spikes sticking up on top of its head. It looks very scary. But don't be afraid! This lizard eats mostly weeds. The lizard does not look very tasty. But other animals think it tastes good. Snakes eat these lizards. So do certain birds. And some people in the rain forest eat them, too! Would you like to eat a lizard for lunch?

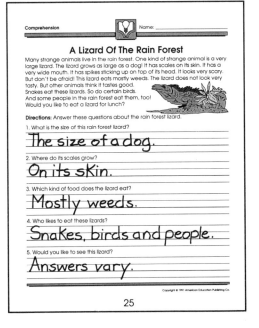

Directions: Answer these questions about the rain forest lizard.

1. What is the size of this rain forest lizard?

The size of a dog.

2. Where do its scales grow?

On its skin.

3. Which kind of food does the lizard eat?

Mostly weeds.

4. Who likes to eat these lizards?

Snakes, birds and people.

5. Would you like to see this lizard?

Answers vary.

25

Birds' Homing Instinct

What is instinct? (Say it this way: in-stinkt.) Instinct is knowing how to do something without being told how. Animals have instincts. Birds have an amazing instinct. It is called the "homing instinct." The homing instinct is the birds' inner urge to find their way somewhere. When birds fly south in the winter, how do they know where to go? How do they know how to get there? When they return in the spring, what makes them return to the same place they left? It is the birds' homing instinct. People do not having a homing instinct. That is why they so often get lost!

Directions: Answer these questions about birds' homing instinct.

1. What word means knowing how to do something without being told?

Instinct.

2. What is the birds' inner urge to find their way somewhere called?

Homing instinct.

3. Which direction do birds fly in the winter?

South.

4. Do people have a homing instinct?

No.

28

Puzzling Out the Homing Instinct

Directions: Re-read the story about birds' homing instinct. Then work the puzzle.

Crossword puzzle:
- W I N T E R (down)
- B I R D S (down)
- I N S T I N C T (across)
- S P R I N G (across)
- P E O P L E (down)
- L O S T (across)

Across
3. Knowing how to do something without being told.
4. This is when birds return from the south.
6. They have no homing instinct, so people get _____.

Down
1. Birds fly south at this time.
2. They have a homing instinct.
5. They do not have a homing instinct.

29

Wouldn't It Be Strange?

Directions: Read the silly poem about what the animals say. Then answer the questions.

Wouldn't it be strange?
Wouldn't you say "Wow!"
If the dog said "moo"
And the cow said "bowwow."
And the cat flew and sang
And the bird said "meow."
Wouldn't it be strange?
Wouldn't you say "Wow!"

1. What strange things would the cat do?
   Fly and sing.

2. What strange thing would the bird do?
   Meow.

3. What strange thing would the cow do?
   Say bow-wow.

4. What strange thing would the dog do?
   Say moo.

32

Comprehension: Pet Crickets

Did you know that some people keep crickets as pets? These people always keep two crickets together. That way, the crickets do not get lonely! The crickets are kept in a flower pot filled with dirt. The dirt helps the crickets feel at home. They are used to being outside. Over the flower pot is a covering that lets air inside. It also keeps the crickets in! Some people use a small net. Other people use cheesecloth. They make sure there is room under the covering for the crickets to hop! Pet crickets like bread and lettuce. They also like raw hamburger meat. Would you like to have a pet cricket?

Directions: Answer these questions about crickets.

1. Where do pet crickets live?
   In flower pots.

2. Why should you put dirt with the crickets?
   To make it look more like their home outside.

3. What is put over the flowerpot?
   A covering. A small net or cheesecloth.

4. Tell 3 things pet crickets like to eat.
   1) Bread 2) Lettuce 3) Raw hamburger meat

30

A Pussy Willow Poem

Directions: Read the poem about the pussy willow plant. Then answer the questions.

I have a little pussy
Her coat is silver gray
She's in a great wide meadow.
She never runs away.
She'll always be a pussy
She'll never be a cat.
'Cause she's a pussy willow!
What do you think of that?

1. Why does a pussy willow never run away?
   Because it is a plant.

2. Why will this pussy never grow to be a cat?
   Because it is a plant and its name is pussy willow. There is no such thing as a "cat willow."

3. Really, what is the "coat of silver gray"?
   It is the color of the plant.

33

More About Crickets

Directions: Read more about crickets. Then work the puzzle.

Only the male cricket can "sing." He "sings" by moving his right wing quickly over his left. It is sort of like playing a violin. The cricket's song is the first insect song we hear in the spring. It is the last insect song we hear in the fall. Crickets do not sing in the winter.

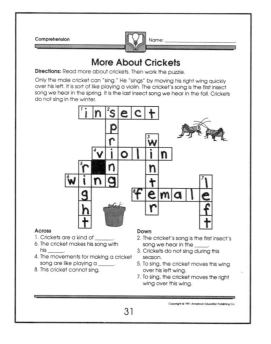

Crossword puzzle:
- I N S E C T (across)
- S P R I N G (down)
- V I O L I N (across)
- W I N T E R (down)
- R I G H T (down)
- W I N G (across)
- F E M A L E (across)
- L E F T (down)

Across
1. Crickets are a kind of _____.
6. The cricket makes his song with his _____.
4. The movements for making a cricket song are like playing a _____.
8. This cricket cannot sing.

Down
2. The cricket's song is the first insect's song we hear in the _____.
3. Crickets do not sing during this season.
5. To sing, the cricket moves this wing over his left wing.
7. To sing, the cricket moves the right wing over this wing.

31

Review

Heather is a beautiful word for a beautiful plant. Some girls are also named Heather. Heather grows high in the mountains of the western United States. It needs very wet ground to grow in. In the high mountains, snow keeps the ground wet enough for heather. It may be as small as 4 inches high. It may grow as high as 12 inches tall. The flowers that grow on heather are a light pinkish-red color. The flowers bloom in June, July and August. Heather is a wild flower. It is one of about 250,000 flowering plants. Have you ever seen a heather plant?

Directions: Answer these questions about heather.

1. Why are some girls named Heather?
   It is a beautiful word.

2. Where in the United States does heather grow?
   In the mountains of the West.

3. The main idea is:
   (Heather is a wild flower that grows in the mountains.)
   Heather is one of 250,000 different kinds of plants.

4. Complete the directions on where in the U.S. to find heather.
   1) Wait until these months to look for heather: June, July and August.
   2) Go to the Mountains out West.
   3) Look for ground that is Very wet.

34

Our Solar System

There are 9 planets in our solar system. All of them circle the sun. The planet closest to the sun is named Mercury. The Greeks said Mercury was the messenger of the gods. The second planet from the sun is named Venus. Venus shines the brightest. Venus was the Greek goddess of beauty. Earth is the third planet from the sun. It is about the same size as Venus.
After Earth is Mars, which is named after the Greek god of War. The other five planets are Jupiter, Saturn, Uranus, Neptune and Pluto. They, too, are named after Greek gods.

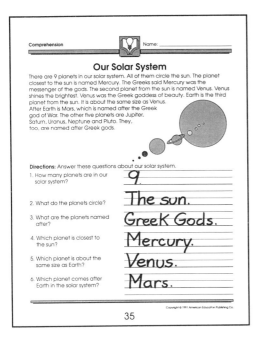

Directions: Answer these questions about our solar system.

1. How many planets are in our solar system?   **9.**

2. What do the planets circle?   **The sun.**

3. What are the planets named after?   **Greek Gods.**

4. Which planet is closest to the sun?   **Mercury.**

5. Which planet is about the same size as Earth?   **Venus.**

6. Which planet comes after Earth in the solar system?   **Mars.**

35

Mars

The U.S. has sent spacecraft to Mars since 1964. There have been many unmanned trips to Mars. ("Unmanned" means there were no people on the spacecraft.) That's why scientists know a lot about this planet. Mars has low temperatures. There is no water on Mars. There is a gas called water vapor. There is also ice on Mars. Scientists have also learned that there is fog on Mars in the early morning! Do you remember when you last saw fog here on Earth? Scientists say the fog on Mars looks the same. As on earth, the fog occurs in low-lying areas of the ground.

Another interesting thing about Mars is that it is very windy. The wind blows up many dust storms on this planet. A spacecraft called Mariner 9 was the first to take picture of dust storms. Later, the unmanned Viking spacecraft landed on the surface of Mars.

Directions: Answer these questions about Mars.

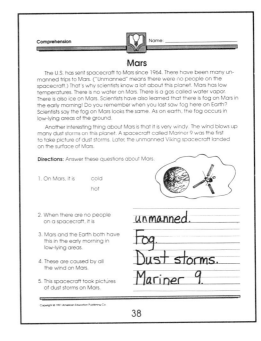

1. On Mars, it is   cold
   hot

2. When there are no people on a spacecraft, it is   **unmanned.**

3. Mars and the Earth both have this in the early morning in low-lying areas.   **Fog.**

4. These are caused by all the wind on Mars.   **Dust storms.**

5. This spacecraft took pictures of dust storms on Mars.   **Mariner 9.**

38

Mercury

In 1974, for the first time a U.S. spacecraft passed within 400 miles of the planet Mercury. The name of the spacecraft was Mariner 10. There were no people on the spacecraft. But there were cameras that could take clear pictures from a long distance. What the pictures showed was interesting. They showed that Mercury's surface was a lot like the surface of the moon. The surface of Mercury is filled with huge holes called craters. A layer of fine dust covers Mercury. This, too, is like the dust on the moon. There is no life on either Mercury or the moon.

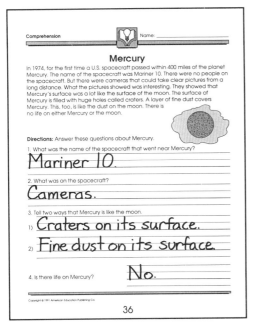

Directions: Answer these questions about Mercury.

1. What was the name of the spacecraft that went near Mercury?

Mariner 10.

2. What was on the spacecraft?

Cameras.

3. Tell two ways that Mercury is like the moon.

1) **Craters on its surface.**

2) **Fine dust on its surface.**

4. Is there life on Mercury?   **No.**

36

Mars

Directions: Re-read the story about Mars. Then work the puzzle.

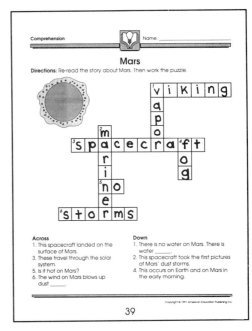

Across
1. This spacecraft landed on the surface of Mars.
3. These travel through the solar system.
5. Is it hot on Mars?
6. The wind on Mars blows up dust _____.

Down
1. There is no water on Mars. There is water _____.
2. This spacecraft took the first pictures of Mars' dust storms.
4. This occurs on Earth and on Mars in the early morning.

39

Venus

For many years, no one knew much about Venus. When people looked through telescopes, they could not see past Venus' clouds. Long ago, people thought the clouds covered living things. Spacecraft radar has shown this is not true. Venus is too hot for life to exist. The temperature on Venus is about 900 degrees! Remember how hot you were the last time it was 90 degrees? Now imagine it being 10 times hotter. Nothing could exist in that heat. It is also very dry on Venus. For life to exist, water must be present. Because of the heat and dryness, we know there are no people, plants or other life on Venus.

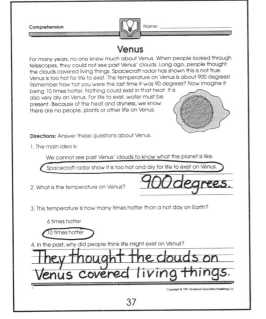

Directions: Answer these questions about Venus.

1. The main idea is:

We cannot see past Venus' clouds to know what the planet is like.

(Spacecraft radar show it is too hot and dry for life to exist on Venus.)

2. What is the temperature on Venus?   **900 degrees.**

3. This temperature is how many times hotter than a hot day on Earth?

6 times hotter

(10 times hotter)

4. In the past, why did people think life might exist on Venus?

They thought the clouds on Venus covered living things.

37

The Rings Of Saturn

Have you looked at Saturn through a strong telescope? If you have, you know it has rings. Saturn is the most beautiful planet to see! It is bright yellow. It is circled by four rings. Two bright rings are on the outside of the circle. Two dark rings are on the inside. The rings of Saturn are made of billions of tiny bits of rocks. The rocks travel around the planet in a swarm. They keep their ring shape as the planet travels around the sun. These rings shine brightly. So does the planet Saturn. Both reflect the rays of the sun. The sun is 885 million miles away from Saturn. It takes Saturn 29 and 1/2 years to travel around the sun!

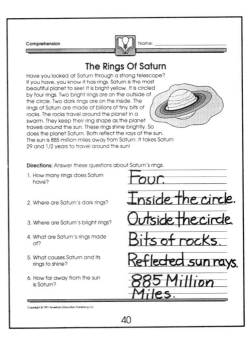

Directions: Answer these questions about Saturn's rings.

1. How many rings does Saturn have?   **Four.**

2. Where are Saturn's dark rings?   **Inside the circle.**

3. Where are Saturn's bright rings?   **Outside the circle.**

4. What are Saturn's rings made of?   **Bits of rocks.**

5. What causes Saturn and its rings to shine?   **Reflected sun rays.**

6. How far away from the sun is Saturn?   **885 Million Miles.**

40

Pluto

Pluto is the ninth planet in our solar system. It is 3,700 million miles from the sun. It cannot be seen from earth without a telescope. Maybe that is why it was named Pluto. Pluto was the Greek god of the dark underworld. For years, scientists suspected there was a ninth planet. But it was not until 1930 that a young scientist proved Pluto existed. His name was Clyde Tombaugh. He compared pictures taken at different times of the sky near Pluto. He noticed one big "star" was in a different place in different pictures. He realized it was not a star. It was a planet moving around the sun.

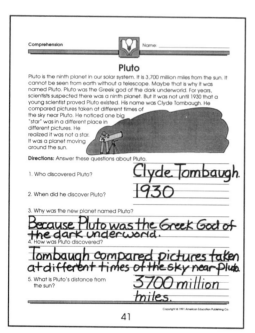

Directions: Answer these questions about Pluto.

1. Who discovered Pluto? **Clyde Tombaugh.**

2. When did he discover Pluto? **1930**

3. Why was the new planet named Pluto? **Because Pluto was the Greek God of the dark underworld.**

4. How was Pluto discovered? **Tombaugh compared pictures taken at different times of the sky near Pluto.**

5. What is Pluto's distance from the sun? **3700 million miles.**

Review

Our moon is not the only moon in the solar system. Some other planets have moons, also. Saturn has 10 moons! Our moon is the Earth's closest neighbor in the solar system. Sometimes our moon is 225,727 miles away. Other times, it is 252,002 miles away. Why? Because the moon revolves around the earth. It does not go around the earth in a perfect circle. So, sometimes its path takes it further away from the earth.

When our astronauts visited the moon, here is what they found: dusty plains, high mountains and huge craters. There is no air or water on the moon. That is why life cannot exist there. The astronauts had to wear space suits to protect their skin from the bright sun. They had to take their own air to breathe. They had to take their own food and water. The moon was an interesting place to visit. But would you want to live there?

Directions: Answer these questions about our moon.

1. The main idea is:

The moon travels around the Earth and the astronauts visited the moon.

⟨ Astronauts found that the moon — Earth's closest neighbor — has no air or water and cannot support life. ⟩

2. Tell 3 things our astronauts found on the moon.

1) **Dusty Plains**   2) **High Mountains**   3) **Huge Craters**

3. Give directions on what to take on a trip to the moon. **A space suit, food, water and air.**

Your Amazing Body

Directions: Read about the human body. Then work the puzzle.

Your body is like an amazing machine. Every minute, your heart pumps six quarts of blood. Your brain sends thousands of messages to the other parts of your body. The messages travel along the nerves at more than 100 miles an hour! Your lungs fill with air. Your ears hear sounds. Your eyes see pictures. And you thought you were just sitting here reading! Your body is always very busy, even when you sleep.

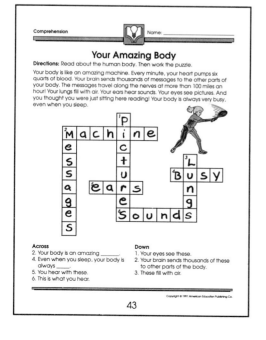

Crossword puzzle:
- 2 Across: MACHINE
- 1 Down: PICTURE
- 3 Down: LUNG
- 3 Across / 5 Across: BUSY
- 4 Across: EARS
- 6 Across: SOUNDS
- 2 Down: MESSAGES

Across
2. Your body is an amazing _____.
4. Even when you sleep, your body is always _____.
5. You hear with these.
6. This is what you hear.

Down
1. Your eyes see these.
2. Your brain sends thousands of these to other parts of the body.
3. These fill with air.

Your Heart

Make your hand into a fist. Now look at it. That is about the size of your heart! Your heart is a strong pump. It works all the time. Right now, it is beating about 90 times a minute. When you run, it beats about 150 times a minute.

Inside, your heart has four spaces. The two spaces on the top are called atria. This is where blood is pumped into the heart. The two spaces on the bottom are called ventricles. This is where blood is pumped out of the heart. The blood is pumped to every part of your body. How? Open and close your fist. See how it tightens and loosens? The heart muscle tightens and loosens, too. This is how it pumps blood.

Directions: Answer these questions about your heart.

1. How often does your heart work? **All the time.**

2. How fast does it beat when you are sitting? **About 90 times a minute.**

3. How fast does it beat when you are running? **About 150 times a minute.**

4. How many spaces are inside your heart? **Four.**

5. What are the heart's upper spaces called? **Atria.**

Your Bones

Are you scared by skeletons? You shouldn't be. There is a skeleton inside you! The skeleton is made up of all the bones in your body. These 206 bones give you your shape. They also protect your heart and everything else inside. Your bones come in many sizes. Some are short. Some are long. Some are rounded. Some are very tiny. The outside of your bones looks solid. Inside, they are filled with something soft. It is called marrow, and it is what keeps your bones alive. Red blood cells and most white blood cells are made here. These cells help to feed the body and fight disease.

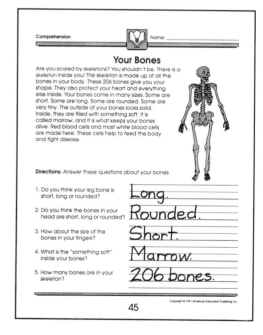

Directions: Answer these questions about your bones.

1. Do you think your leg bone is short, long or rounded? **Long.**

2. Do you think the bones in your head are short, long or rounded? **Rounded.**

3. How about the size of the bones in your fingers? **Short.**

4. What is the "something soft" inside your bones? **Marrow.**

5. How many bones are in your skeleton? **206 bones.**

Your Muscles

Can you make a fist? You could not do this without muscles. You need muscles to make your body move. You have muscles everywhere. There are muscles in your legs. There are even muscles in your tongue!

Remember, your heart is a muscle. It is called an "involuntary muscle" because it works without help from you. Your stomach muscles are also involuntary. You don't need to tell your stomach to digest food. Other muscles are called "voluntary muscles." You must tell these muscles to move. Most voluntary muscles are hooked to bones. When the muscles squeeze, they cause the bone to move. Without your muscles, you would be nothing but a "bag of bones!"

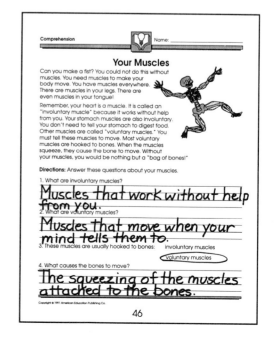

Directions: Answer these questions about your muscles.

1. What are involuntary muscles? **Muscles that work without help from you.**

2. What are voluntary muscles? **Muscles that move when your mind tells them to.**

3. These muscles are usually hooked to bones: involuntary muscles

⟨ Voluntary muscles ⟩

4. What causes the bones to move? **The squeezing of the muscles attached to the bones.**

More About Your Muscles

Directions: Read more about your muscles. Then work the puzzle.

Did you know your muscles have names? No, their names are not Jason or Andrea! Their names have to do with their jobs. The muscles that pull your forearms down are called triceps. "Tri" means three. The triceps have three parts of muscle working together. The muscles that pull your forearms up are called biceps. "Bi" means two. The biceps have two parts of muscle working together. Each set of muscles has a certain job to do. Muscles in the front of the foot pull your toes up. Muscles on the back of the thighs bend your knees. Aren't you glad you have muscles?

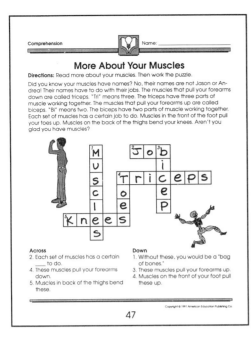

Across
2. Each set of muscles has a certain _____ to do.
4. These muscles pull your forearms down.
5. Muscles in back of the thighs bend these.

Down
1. Without these, you would be a "bag of bones."
3. These muscles pull your forearms up.
4. Muscles on the front of your foot pull these up.

47

Review

When you are grown, your brain will weigh only three pounds. But what an important three pounds! Billions of brain cells are packed into your brain. The cells make up the three areas of the brain. One part does your thinking and feeling. Another part of the brain helps you move your body. It also helps you keep your balance. A third part of the brain keeps you alive!
It keeps your heart beating and your lungs working so you don't have to think about these things. This part of your brain is called the medulla. (Say it this way: ma-dool-la.) As long as you are alive, the medulla never rests.

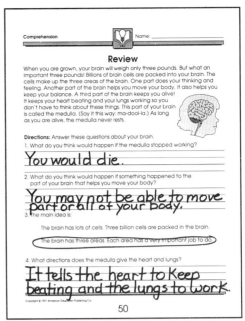

Directions: Answer these questions about your brain.

1. What do you think would happen if the medulla stopped working?

You would die.

2. What do you think would happen if something happened to the part of your brain that helps you move your body?

You may not be able to move part or all of your body.

3. The main idea is:

The brain has lots of cells. Three billion cells are packed in the brain.

(The brain has three areas. Each area has a very important job to do.)

4. What directions does the medulla give the heart and lungs?

It tells the heart to keep beating and the lungs to work.

50

Your Hands

Wiggle your fingers. That was easy, wasn't it? Now clap your hands! Good job. But it wasn't as easy as you think! Each of your hands has 27 bones. Eight of the 27 bones are in your wrist. There are five bones in each of your palms. Your hands have many muscles, too. It took 30 muscles to wiggle your fingers. When you use your hands, the bones and muscles work together. Remember this the next time you cut your meat. You will use your wrist bones and muscles. You will use your finger bones and muscles. Cutting your meat seems easy. And it is — thanks to your muscles and bones!

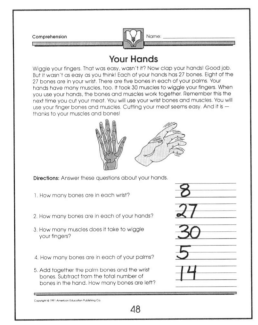

Directions: Answer these questions about your hands.

1. How many bones are in each wrist? **8**

2. How many bones are in each of your hands? **27**

3. How many muscles does it take to wiggle your fingers? **30**

4. How many bones are in each of your palms? **5**

5. Add together the palm bones and the wrist bones. Subtract from the total number of bones in the hand. How many bones are left? **14**

48

Searching For Ways To Travel

Directions: There are many ways to get from one place to another. Read the clues and fill in the blanks with your answers. Then circle the 8 things you can use for travel in the word search. The words may go up, down or sideways.

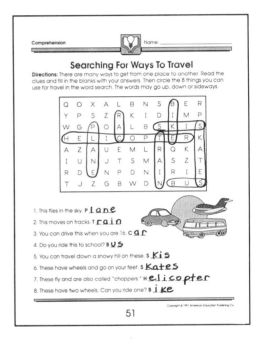

Q	O	X	A	L	B	X	D	M	P
Y	P	S	Z	R	K	I	D	I	M
W	G	P	O	A	L	B	S	K	I	S
H	E	L	I	C	O	P	T	E	R	K
A	Z	A	U	E	M	L	R	Q	K	A
I	U	N	J	T	S	M	A	S	Z	T
R	D	E	N	P	D	N	I	R	I	E
T	J	Z	G	B	W	D	N	B	U	S

1. This flies in the sky. P **l a n e**
2. This moves on tracks. T **r a i n**
3. You can drive this when you are 16. C **a r**
4. Do you ride this to school? B **U S**
5. You can travel down a snowy hill on these. S **K i s**
6. These have wheels and go on your feet. S **K a t e s**
7. These fly and are also called "choppers." H **e l i c o p t e r**
8. These have two wheels. Can you ride one? B **i K e**

51

Your Lungs

Imagine millions of teeny-tiny balloons joined together. That is what your lungs are like. When you breathe, the air goes to your two lungs. One is located on each side of your chest. The heart is located between the two lungs. The lungs are soft, spongy and delicate. That is why there are bones around the lungs. These bones are called the rib cage. The rib cage protects the lungs so they can do their job. The lungs bring oxygen into the body. (Say it this way: ox-ee-gin.) They also take a waste out of the body. This waste is called carbon dioxide. We could not live without our lungs!

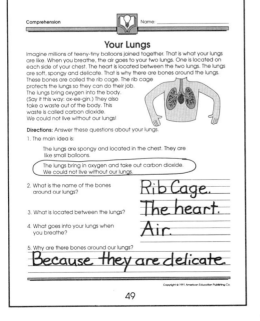

Directions: Answer these questions about your lungs.

1. The main idea is:

The lungs are spongy and located in the chest. They are like small balloons.

(The lungs bring in oxygen and take out carbon dioxide. We could not live without our lungs.)

2. What is the name of the bones around our lungs? **Rib Cage.**

3. What is located between the lungs? **The heart.**

4. What goes into your lungs when you breathe? **Air.**

5. Why are there bones around our lungs? **Because they are delicate.**

49

The Horseless Carriage

Do you know how people traveled before cars? They rode horses! Often the horses were hooked up to wagons. Some horses were hooked up to carriages. Wagons were used to carry supplies. Carriages had covered tops. They were used to carry people. Both wagons and carriages were pulled by horses.

The first cars in the United States were invented shortly before the year 1900. These cars looked a lot like carriages. The seats were high off the ground. They had very thin wheels. The difference was they were powered by engines. Carriages were pulled by horses. Still, they looked alike. People called the first cars "horseless carriages."

Directions: Answer these questions about "horseless carriages."

1. Tell a way wagons and carriages were the same.

Both were pulled by horses.

2. When were the first cars invented?

Before 1900.

3. Why were they called horseless carriages?

They had high seats and thin wheels.

4. What was the difference between a carriage and a horseless carriage?

One pulled by horse, other powered by engine.

52

The Horseless Carriage

Directions: Read more about the first cars. Then work the puzzle.

Can you guess how many cars there were in the United States 95 years ago? Only four! Today, nearly every family has a car. Most families have two cars. Henry Ford started the Ford Motor Company in 1903. His first cars were called the Model T. People thought cars would never be used in place of horses. Ford had to sell his cars through department stores! Soon, cars became "the thing." By 1920, there were 200 different U.S. companies making cars!

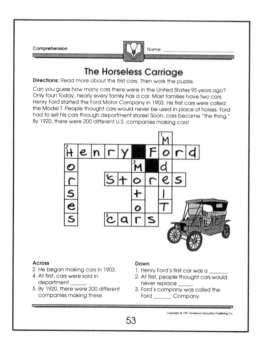

Across
2. He began making cars in 1903.
4. At first, cars were sold in department _____.
5. By 1920, there were 200 different companies making these.

Down
1. Henry Ford's first car was a _____.
2. At first, people thought cars would never replace _____.
3. Ford's company was called the Ford _____ Company.

53

The First Trains

Trains have been around much longer than cars or trucks. The first train used by America was made in England. It was brought to the U.S. in 1829. Because it was light green, it was nicknamed "the Grasshopper." Unlike a real grasshopper, this train was not fast. It only went 10 miles an hour.

That same year, another train was built by an American. Compared to the Grasshopper, the American train was fast. It went 30 miles an hour. People were amazed. This train was called the Rocket. Can you guess why?

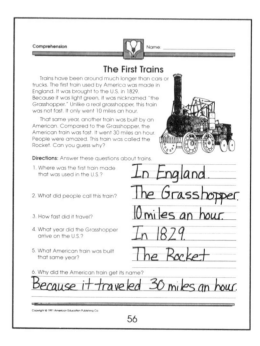

Directions: Answer these questions about trains.

1. Where was the first train made that was used in the U.S.?
   In England.

2. What did people call this train?
   The Grasshopper.

3. How fast did it travel?
   10 miles an hour.

4. What year did the Grasshopper arrive on the U.S.?
   In 1829.

5. What American train was built that same year?
   The Rocket

6. Why did the American train get its name?
   Because it traveled 30 miles an hour.

56

A Giant Snowblower

A snowblower is used to blow snow off sidewalks and driveways. It is faster than using a shovel. It is also easier! Airports use snowblowers, too. They use them to clear the runways that planes use. Many airports use a giant snowblower. It is a type of truck. This snowblower weighs 30,000 pounds! It can blow 100,000 pounds of snow every minute. It cuts through the snow with huge blades. The blades are over six feet tall.

Directions: Answer these questions about the big trucks.

1. Why do people use snowblowers instead of shovels?
   They are faster and easier.

2. What do airports use snowblowers for?
   To clear runways for planes.

3. How much do some airport snowblowers weigh?
   30,000 pounds.

4. How much snow can it blow every minute?
   100,000 pounds of snow.

5. What does the snowblower use to cut through snow?
   High blades over six feet tall.

54

The First Trains

Directions: Re-read the story of the first trains. Read the clues and fill in the blanks below with your answer. Now, find and circle these words in the word search.

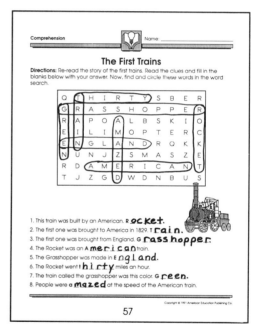

1. This train was built by an American. R **ocket**.
2. The first one was brought to America in 1829. T **rain**.
3. The first one was brought from England. G **rasshopper**.
4. The Rocket was an A **merican** train.
5. The Grasshopper was made in E **ngland**.
6. The Rocket went t **hirty** miles an hour.
7. The train called the grasshopper was this color. G **reen**.
8. People were a **mazed** at the speed of the American train.

57

Early Trucks

What would we do without trucks? Your family may not own a truck. But everyone depends on trucks. Trucks bring our food to stores. Trucks deliver our new clothes to shopping centers. The goods of the world move on trucks.

Trucks are harder to make than cars. They must be sturdy. They carry heavy loads. They cannot break down. The first trucks were on the roads in 1900. Like trains, they were powered by steam engines. They did not use gasoline. The first trucks did not have heavy wheels. Their engines broke down. Trucks changed when the U.S. entered World War I in 1917. Big, heavy tires were put on trucks. Gasoline engines were used. Trucks used in war had to be sturdy. Lives were at stake!

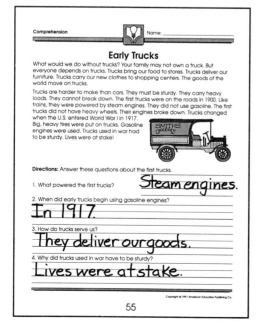

Directions: Answer these questions about the first trucks.

1. What powered the first trucks?
   Steam engines.

2. When did early trucks begin using gasoline engines?
   In 1917.

3. How do trucks serve us?
   They deliver our goods.

4. Why did trucks used in war have to be sturdy?
   Lives were at stake.

55

Review

Trains are noisy! It is hard to hear around trains. That is why hand signals are used. The signals tell the engineer who drives the train many things. There is a signal to tell him to stop completely. Another signal tells him to reduce his speed. Other signals tell the engineer to proceed, apply brakes, release brakes, back up. These six signals are very important.

During daylight, the signals are made with a white or red kerchief. At night, the signals are made with a big lantern that can be seen easily. A "signal man" moves the lantern. The arrows in the pictures show which way the lantern is moved.

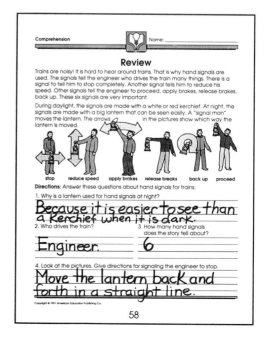

stop   reduce speed   apply brakes   release breaks   back up   proceed

Directions: Answer these questions about hand signals for trains.

1. Why is a lantern used for hand signals at night?
   Because it is easier to see than a kerchief when it is dark.

2. Who drives the train?
   Engineer.

3. How many hand signals does the story tell about?
   6

4. Look at the pictures. Give directions for signaling the engineer to stop.
   Move the lantern back and forth in a straight line.

58

82

Rhinos

Rhinos are the second-largest land animal. Only elephants are bigger.

Most people think rhinos are ugly. Their full name is "rhinoceros" (rhy-noss-ur-us). There are five kinds of rhinos: square-lipped rhino, black rhino, Great Indian rhino, Sumatran rhino (say it this way: sue-ma-trahn) and Javan rhino.

Rhinos have a very good sense of smell. It also helps protect them. They can smell other animals far away. They don't eat them, though. Rhinos do not eat meat. They are vegetarians. (Say it this way: veg-e-tair-ee-uns.)

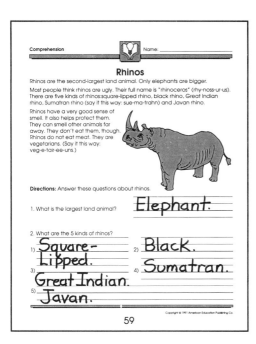

Directions: Answer these questions about rhinos.

1. What is the largest land animal? **Elephant.**

2. What are the 5 kinds of rhinos?
   1) **Square-Lipped.**
   2) **Black.**
   3) **Great Indian.**
   4) **Sumatran.**
   5) **Javan.**

59

Rodents

You are surrounded by rodents (row-dents)! There are 1,500 different kinds of rodents. One of the most common rodents is the mouse. Rats, gophers (go-furs) and beavers are rodents. So are squirrels and porcupines (pork-ya-pines).

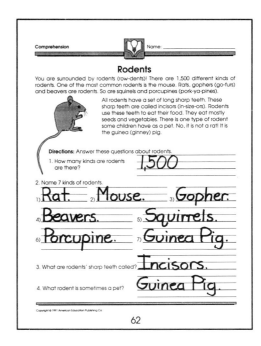

All rodents have a set of long sharp teeth. These sharp teeth are called incisors (in-size-ors). Rodents use these teeth to eat their food. They eat mostly seeds and vegetables. There is one type of rodent some children have as a pet. No, it is not a rat! It is the guinea (ginney) pig.

Directions: Answer these questions about rodents.

1. How many kinds are rodents are there? **1,500**

2. Name 7 kinds of rodents.
   1) **Rat.** 2) **Mouse.** 3) **Gopher.**
   4) **Beavers.** 5) **Squirrels.**
   6) **Porcupine.** 7) **Guinea Pig.**

3. What are rodents' sharp teeth called? **Incisors.**

4. What rodent is sometimes a pet? **Guinea Pig.**

62

Robins

Have you ever heard this old song? "Oh, the red, red robin, goes bob-bob-bobbin along!" It is hard not to smile when you see a robin. Robins were first called "redbreasts." If you have seen one, you know why! The fronts of their bodies are red. Robins are cheerful-looking birds.

Robins sing a sweet, mellow song. That is another reason people like robins. The female robin lays two to six eggs. She sits on them for two weeks. Then the father and the mother robin both bring food to the baby birds. Robins eat spiders, worms, insects and small seeds. Robins will also eat food scraps people put out for them.

Directions: Answer these questions about robins.

1. Name one reason people like robins.
   They sing a sweet, mellow song.

2. How many eggs does a mother robin lay?
   From two to six.

3. What do robins eat?
   Spiders, worms, insects, small seeds and food scraps.

4. Who sits on the robin eggs?
   Mother Robin.

60

A Puzzle For The Birds

Directions: Re-read the story about robins. Then work the puzzle.

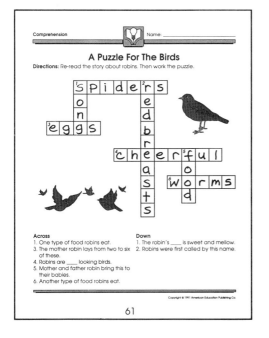

Crossword answers:
- ¹spiders
- ²on
- ³eggs
- ⁴redbreasts (down)
- ⁵cheerful
- ⁶food (down)
- ⁷worms

Across
1. One type of food robins eat.
3. The mother robin lays from two to six of these.
4. Robins are ____ looking birds.
5. Mother and father robin bring this to their babies.
6. Another type of food robins eat.

Down
1. The robin's ____ is sweet and mellow.
2. Robins were first called by this name.

61

Sheep

Sheep like to stay close together. They do not run off. They move together in a flock. They live on sheep ranches. Some sheep grow 20 pounds of fleece each year. After it is cut off, the fleece is called wool. Cutting off the wool is called "shearing." It does not hurt the sheep to be sheared. The wool is very warm and is used to make clothing.

Female sheep are called ewes ("yous"). Some types of ewes have only one baby each year. The baby is called a lamb. Other types of ewes have two or three lambs each year.

Directions: Answer these questions about sheep.

1. Why is sheep's behavior helpful to sheep ranchers?
   They do not run off.

2. Would you rather own the kind of sheep that has one baby each year? Or would you rather have the kind that has two or three babies?
   The kind that has two or three.

3. Why?
   The more sheep you have, the more wool you will get.

4. When it is still on the sheep, what is wool called? **Fleece.**

5. What is a group of sheep called? **Flock.**

63

Review

Have you ever smelled a skunk? A skunk's odor helps to protect him. The smell comes from scent (sent) glands under the skunk's tail. These scent glands make a liquid (lick quid) that smells very bad. The skunk can shoot the liquid 10 feet into the air. The skunk shoots it to protect itself. The skunk arches its back before it shoots.

There are 10 types of skunks. The most common type is black. It has a white strip down its head and back. It has a black tip to its tail. Some people have skunks for pets. What do you think they have removed from the skunk first?

Directions: Answer these questions about skunks.

1. Give directions on what to do to have a skunk for a pet.
   Have the scent glands removed.

2. What would you do if you saw a wild skunk arch its back?
   Get away!

3. Why?
   It's getting ready to shoot its scent.

4. How many types of skunks are there? **10**

64

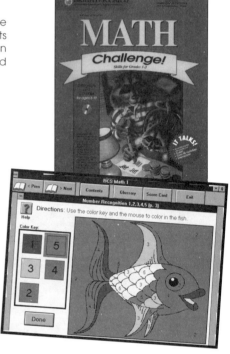
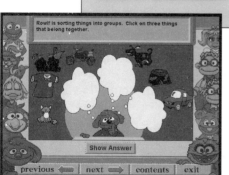
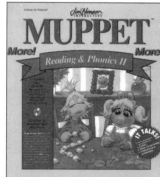

OVERVIEW

ENRICHMENT READING is designed to provide children with practice in reading and to increase students' reading abilities. The program consists of six editions, one each for grades 1 through 6. The major areas of reading instruction—word skills, vocabulary, study skills, comprehension, and literary forms—are covered as appropriate at each level.

ENRICHMENT READING provides a wide range of activities that target a variety of skills in each instructional area. The program is unique because it helps children expand their skills in playful ways with games, puzzles, riddles, contests, and stories. The high-interest activities are informative and fun to do.

Home involvement is important to any child's success in school. *ENRICHMENT READING* is the ideal vehicle for fostering home involvement. Every lesson provides specific opportunities for children to work with a parent, a family member, an adult, or a friend.

AUTHORS

Peggy Kaye, the author of *ENRICHMENT READING*, is also an author of *ENRICHMENT MATH* and the author of two parent/teacher resource books, *Games for Reading* and *Games for Math*. Currently, Ms. Kaye divides her time between writing books and tutoring students in reading and math. She has also taught for ten years in New York City public and private schools.

WRITERS

Timothy J. Baehr is a writer and editor of instructional materials on the elementary, secondary, and college levels. Mr. Baehr has also authored an award-winning column on bicycling and a resource book for writers of educational materials.

Cynthia Benjamin is a writer of reading instructional materials, television scripts, and original stories. Ms. Benjamin has also tutored students in reading at the New York University Reading Institute.

Russell Ginns is a writer and editor of materials for a children's science and nature magazine. Mr. Ginn's speciality is interactive materials, including games, puzzles, and quizzes.

WHY ENRICHMENT READING?

Enrichment and parental involvement are both crucial to children's success in school, and educators recognize the important role work done at home plays in the educational process. Enrichment activities give children opportunities to practice, apply, and expand their reading skills, while encouraging them to think while they read. *ENRICHMENT READING* offers exactly this kind of opportunity. Each lesson focuses on an important reading skill and involves children in active learning. Each lesson will entertain and delight children.

When childen enjoy their lessons and are involved in the activities, they are naturally alert and receptive to learning. They understand more. They remember more. All children enjoy playing games, having contests, and solving puzzles. They like reading interesting stories, amusing stories, jokes, and riddles. Activities such as these get children involved in reading. This is why these kinds of activities form the core of *ENRICHMENT READING*.

Each lesson consists of two parts. Children complete the first part by themselves. The second part is completed together with a family member, an adult, or a friend. *ENRICHMENT READING* activities do not require people at home to teach reading. Instead, the activities involve everyone in enjoyable reading games and interesting language experiences.

Page 65   *Entry words:* rose, rabbit, fox, piano, lake, baseball

Page 66   *Changed words:* <u>beautiful</u>–ugly, <u>everyone</u>–no one or nobody, <u>sweet</u>–sour, <u>boys</u>–girls, <u>walk</u>–run, <u>backwards</u>–forwards, <u>whisper</u>–shout or yell, <u>girls</u>–boys, <u>big</u>–little or small, <u>long</u>–short, <u>never</u>–always, <u>remember</u>–forget, <u>won't</u>–will, <u>come</u>–leave or go, <u>here</u>–there, <u>out</u>–in; answers will vary

Page 67   here, blew, see, tail, won, new, weigh, waist; 20 + 25 + 25 + 15 + 30 + 25 + 20 + 15 = 175; 175

Page 68

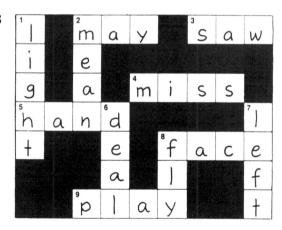

ENRICHMENT ANSWER KEY
Reading Grade 3

Page 69   Answers and results will vary.

Page 70   Answers will vary.

Page 71   Plan 2 is in correct order; 2

Page 72   All the statements are true.